D0667907

Shine On, Star of Bethlehem

A worship resource for Advent, Christmas and Epiphany

Compiled by Geoffrey Duncan

THE
PILGRIM
PRESS
Cleveland

Published in the USA and Canada by
The Pilgrim Press
700 Prospect Avenue East, Cleveland, Ohio 44115-1100
pilgrimpress.com

Originally published in 2001 by
The Canterbury Press Norwich
St Mary's Works, St Mary's Plain
Norwich, Norfolk NR3 3BH

All rights reserved. No part of this publication which is
copyright may be reproduced, stored in a retrieval
system or transmitted, in any form or by any means,
electronic, mechanical, photocopying, recording, or
otherwise, without the prior permission of the publisher.

© 2002 Geoffrey Duncan

The editors and contributors assert their rights under the
Copyright, Design and Patents Act, 1988, to be
identified as the authors of this Work.

ISBN 0-8298-1513-9

The Pilgrim Press edition published 2002. All rights reserved.

06 05 04 03 02   5 4 3 2 1

A catalogue record for this book is available
from the Library of Congress.

Typeset by Rowland Phototypesetting Limited,
Bury St Edmunds, Suffolk
Printed and bound in Great Britain

Contents

Introduction

Christmas is a time for tradition. People who rarely go to a church at other times of the year still flock to the familiar services of nine lessons and carols and midnight Communion. Nativity plays are as popular as ever, as is carol singing in the streets or in local pubs and community centres. Yet there is also room for a little novelty at Christmas. People come to these events conscious of injustice and inequality in our world and of the increasing gulf between the simplicity of Christ's birth at Bethlehem and the glittering commercialism of today's celebrations. Their concerns cry out to be reflected in Christmas worship, yet it is not always easy to find the means to do this.

For a number of years Christian Aid has produced worship materials for Christmas which aim to convey something of the reality of life for people in different parts of the developing world. Sometimes these have focused on our partner organisations, such as the Movement of the Landless in Brazil, and some of that material is included here (as on page 131–33 for example). Sometimes we have simply offered new words to familiar carols, such as Rebecca Dudley's version of 'Away in a manger' (page 190). Items like this can very easily be incorporated into even the most traditional of services.

Much in this new anthology can be used in private reflection or in informal small group worship. Geoffrey Duncan has taken work by Christian Aid writers as a starting point and incorporated more items from across the world, from Europe to the Antipodes, via the Americas, Africa and Asia. His collection covers the Advent season, Christmas and Epiphany, and will be a source of delight to people browsing at home and a godsend to busy worship-leaders.

The various elements that make up this anthology can

hardly fail to remind us that in public and private worship, we are uniting our prayers with Christians of many cultures and traditions, whose situation is very different from our own. And as Christian Aid works with partner organisations overseas for justice, peace and the eradication of poverty, we are conscious that at Christmastime we are further united by Christian hope: the hope which, to paraphrase St John, is to be found in the light that shines in the darkness and which the darkness has never overcome.

Daleep Mukarji
Director, Christian Aid

Part One:
Advent

Holy One, we wait for you . . .

The Promise

The Sprouting of a New Branch

Based on Isaiah 11:1–10

To open worship

Voice 1 At last a branch sprouts!

Voice 2 *Don't be silly, this tree is dead.*

Voice 1 Hurray, the expected one is here!

Voice 2 *What's all the fuss, it will be ages yet.*

Voice 1 Great news, the poor will be treated fairly!

Voice 2 *Huh, the poor should get on and help themselves.*

Voice 1 Look, people are being fair to each other!

Voice 2 *What, has everyone gone soft or something?*

Voice 1 Rejoice, all creation is able to live together: wolves and lambs, calves and lions!

Voice 2 *You're mad, the strong are just waiting for a chance to take advantage of the weak ones.*

Voice 1 See there, children playing in dangerous places are unharmed!

Voice 2 *Yeah, for how long – it will end in tears, mark my words.*

Voice 3 (from far away) **Just as the water fills the sea, the land will be filled with people who know and honour the Lord.**

Janet Lees

3

The New Branch

(Jeremiah 33:14–15)

God says
We're opening a new Branch
a new Partnership with people.
Israel and Judah will benefit
(it's in the terms of the contract)
Safe cities, peaceful communities
the new Branch will see to it.
Its mission will be based on just dealing
(just like the Parent company but
with a local focus)
and in time
everyone will know that this new Branch
expresses and shares the Name of God
'the Lord our Righteousness'.

God of all creative enterprise
wherever companies and communities
are planning new ventures in partnership,
let the longing for justice drive their negotiations
and peace and safety be their prime concerns.
Help us and them to see
in their meetings and papers
their setbacks and achievements
the coming of God our Righteousness
whose love and justice
have always been
will always be
written into your covenant agreement
with humankind.

Heather Pencavel

In Due Time

God's due time,
    not our immediate now,
God's perfect timing,
    not ours of impatience.
God's timetable,
    not our schedule,
God's will,
    not our self will.
God's completion,
    not our imperfect incompleteness.
God's day of salvation,
    not our day of self effort.
God's finale celebrations,
    not our man-made festivities.
God's delivery date,
    not our probable date.
God's due time,
    not ours to disagree about.

God's time is now due!

Frances Ballantyne

Bring Peace

God our Father, you spoke to the prophets of old of a Saviour
who would bring peace. You helped them to spread the joyful
message of his coming kingdom. Help us, as we prepare to
celebrate his birth, to share with those around us the good
news of your power and love. We ask this through Jesus
Christ, the Light who is coming into the world.

Michael Perham

A Time of Hope

It seemed as though the world stood still
when neighbours turned on neighbours,
burning houses, killing men and women,
sadly, so terribly, targeting children,
well might they think that hope had ended –
yet He is coming.

What is left to celebrate
when your parents have been killed before your eyes,
when your children have been slaughtered
by those you thought your friends,
when your arms show the marks of the machete?
Yet He is coming.

Who is there to worship
when one church has been burned to the ground,
when another church has become the tomb of former
    worshippers,
where acts of treachery have filled the nave
and violence has surrounded the altar
and the cries of slain infants still hang in the air?

It seemed as though Rwanda could not celebrate again,
as though the faith of the people had been for ever crushed,
as though the priests and pastors could no longer preach,
as though the hymns were silenced by the genocide
and the hopes of the people had forever perished
in the maelstrom of a world gone mad.
Yet He is coming
and the Advent praise rises from a people
who know in their hearts that His light shines
and the darkness will never overcome it.

John Johansen-Berg

Heralds of Good News

A Voice Crying in the Wilderness

There's a voice crying in the wilderness,
up and down the high street,
through the railway arches.
The voice says 'Get ready for God!

'Make the path straight,
repair the potholes and pavement cracks,
fill in the ditches,
cultivate the waste land.
The mountains and the hills,
empty office blocks
and power towers will be laid low.
Those bent over and weighed down
will rise up and everyone will recognise
God's handiwork.'
Praise God!

Janet Lees

'After Me Comes Another ...'

A voice and a vision,
A man from the wilderness,
The wandering prophet
Of God's appointed hour.
In each generation
God fulfils His purpose,
So shall all behold him –
His justice and His power.

A voice in the desert,
Proclaiming the Kingdom,
The long-awaited Jesus,
Whose love will break the law –
Deaf ears will hear laughter
From the lips of silence;
Light for those in darkness,
And good news to the poor.

The waiting is ended,
God's sign has been given,
On his beloved Son,
His Spirit has been poured;
Behold, the Lamb of God,
Sacrifice and Saviour;
God's will now made perfect
In Jesus Christ, our Lord.

Jill Jenkins

Voices

A reflection on Isaiah 40

A voice
howling in the night wolf's hunger
screaming in the cry of the owl
in the squeal of the beast
dying under the predator's claw
in the wail of the wind
whistling in the wilderness
'Here is where God will come!
this will be a road for our God.'

a voice
singing in the mother's lullaby
comfort, comfort
tenderly spoken for pains past,
soothing the hurt

8

all over now
all done.

a voice
calling from the high place
God, God alone
is constant,
God speaks always
the word for the time
tender as a shepherd
when the lambs are weak
the ewes weary;
stern as the Judge
pronouncing sentence
for the squandering of creation.

a voice
howling in the night wolf's hunger
screaming in the cry of the owl
in the squeal of the beast
dying under the predator's claw
in the wail of the wind
whistling in the wilderness
'Here is where God will come!
this will be a road for our God.'

God we hear you
in the dark, desolate place
in the quiet intimate place
on the high hill and deep in the heart
crying out
comforting
calling
challenging
we hear you
we hear you.
Amen.

Heather Pencavel

9

To a World so Torn and Tortured

To a world so torn and tortured
Came the voice of one who knew
What it cost to lift oppression,
Challenge the accepted view.

John convicted crowds before him,
Charged hypocrisy with God;
Opened up the way for Jesus
Who would follow where he trod.

Then imprisoned, John was silenced;
Yet a voice more powerful still
Challenged in and out of season
All who heard to do God's will.

Living Christ would lift oppression,
Dying he would seem to fail;
Crying out in desolation,
Yet God's love would still prevail.

Tune: 8.7.8.7

Andrew Pratt

Roadbuilding

Luke 3:1–6

Roadbuilding is rough work
hard labour, muscles strained
hands calloused, back near breaking
even with lifting gear, hard hat, protective boots.

Site clearance is dirty work
and dangerous
removing rotten structures,

risking unsafe ground
uncovering long-forgotten corruption,
the stink too strong to breathe
of waste and dereliction.

God you cry out to us
to clear the site, build the road
because you are coming
and you will come
along the road we build.

Give your people, we pray
the will and stamina for the job.
Give us courage, to tackle the clearance
of debt and exploitation
which corrupt communities and nations.
Give us the grit and determination
to straighten out the crooked structures
which make it hard for the poor and the weak
to journey to freedom –
And help us to shout aloud that you will come
along the road we build.

Heather Pencavel

Telling It Like It Is

Luke 3:7–18

Hellfire preaching
Uncompromising demands
straight talk – that's John,
telling it like it is.
Sometimes it all seems very simple:
God reigns, God judges
which means
just sharing of property

11

honest trade
no bullying, no blackmail
no greed. Simple enough.
If only . . .

God you are coming to your people
to reign with justice.
Help us to recognise your coming
in fair trade campaigns
in consultations between management and workers;
in power structures which put human wellbeing
as their first priority.

Reigning, judging God,
come today to our world of trade
and show us how to make it fair;
come to our industry and work through us
to create fulfilling work and fair conditions;
come to our authority structures
and show us how to blend mercy with justice.

Let your reign of justice begin today.

Heather Pencavel

Our God Is a Biased God

With justice he will judge the poor and defend the humble
(Isaiah 11:4)
Prove your repentance by the fruit you bear (Matthew 3:8)

The voice which cries
in our own particular wilderness
calls for a change in the way
we see and value things
in our high production,
high consumption society;
in our success driven world.

12

Our God is a biased God,
biased in favour of the poor and needy;
biased in favour of the misfits,
the rejects,
the rebels;
biased in favour of the people
who've made a thorough mess of their lives.
And the voice cries:
'Will you not see them as I see them?'
'Will you not care for them as I care?'

Lord,
if you discount parking and speeding offences
we're a pretty law-abiding group of people,
but,
at times,
you do give us the uncomfortable feeling
that being law-abiding isn't quite enough.
Help us to better understand
what you mean by righteousness and justice.
Help us to make your values our values,
and strengthen our will
to witness and work for your ways
by the things we count important
and the manner in which
we live our everyday lives.

Edmund Banyard

Waiting and Watching

Holy One

Holy One,
we wait for you
to come to us again,
baby-small and vulnerable,
to grace our poverty,
our humanity
with a heart beat,
a breath and a cry.

Holy One,
you wait for us
to notice you again,
baby-small and vulnerable,
here in these people
and in this place,
present in a heart beat,
a breath and a cry.

May the guiding Spirit
once again bring your waiting
and our waiting together,
to lift up the vulnerable,
and confirm the beauty of our humanity,
each heart beat,
every breath and cry
bringing to birth renewed lives
filled with everlasting hope.

Janet Lees

14

Our Hope and Our Desire

God, our hope and our desire,
we wait for your coming
as a woman longs for the birth,
the exile for her home,
the lover for the touch of his beloved,
and the humble poor for justice.

Janet Morley

Coming for You, Coming for Me

All the broken hearts
shall rejoice:
all those who are heavy laden,
whose eyes are tired
and do not see,
shall be lifted up
to meet with
the motherly healer.
The battered souls and bodies
shall be healed;
the hungry
shall be fed;
the imprisoned
shall be free;
all her earthly children
shall regain joy
in the reign
of the just and loving one
coming for you
coming for me
in this time
in this world.

Sun Ai Lee Park
Hong Kong/USA

God of the Poor

God of the poor,
we long to meet you
yet almost miss you;
we strive to help you
yet only discover our need.
Interrupt our comfort
with your nakedness,
touch our possessiveness
with your poverty,
and surprise our guilt
with the grace of your welcome
in Jesus Christ, **Amen**

Janet Morley

Advent

The sun has dimmed its dazzling rays,
The daylight reached its shortest span;
Now all the hushed and humbled earth
Awaits the birth of God made man.

How can we face this tiny judge
Who found no lodging at our inn,
But by a silent glance of love
Pronounces freedom from our sin?

Like nature in these Advent days
We must put off our lofty pride,
In stillness and humility
Prepare our hearts for Christmastide.

Praise to the Father, by whose plan
Our Saviour came to set us free,

Praise to the Son and Paraclete
Who joins us to the Trinity.
Amen

Order of the Holy Paraclete

For the Darkness and the Light

For the darkness of waiting
of not knowing what is to come
of staying ready and quiet and attentive,
we praise you, O God:

**For the darkness and the light
are both alike to you.**

For the darkness of staying silent
for the terror of having nothing to say
and for the greater terror
of needing to say nothing,
we praise you, O God:

**For the darkness and the light
are both alike to you.**

For the darkness of loving
in which it is safe to surrender
to let go of our self-protection
and to stop holding back our desire,
we praise you, O God:

**For the darkness and the light
are both alike to you.**

For the darkness of choosing
when you give us the moment
to speak, and act, and change,
and we cannot know what we have set in motion

but we still have to take the risk,
we praise you, O God:

**For the darkness and the light
are both alike to you.**

For the darkness of hoping
in a world which longs for you,
for the wrestling and the labouring of all creation
we praise you, O God:

**For the darkness and the light
are both alike to you.**

Janet Morley

May the Light of Justice Shine

Where people are denied dignity of name and culture;
abused, ridiculed or subtly excluded:
where race or class or gender
are used to deny rights and liberty:
  **God our hope and our deliverer,
  shatter the rod of prejudice
  and let your light bring freedom to our darkness.**

Where the prosperous profit from the poor
and families are caught in the spiral of debt;
where men are deprived of work and role
and women's labour is underpaid or invisible:
  **God our hope and our deliverer,
  shatter the rod of poverty
  and let your light bring justice to our darkness.**

Where the strong bully and harass the weak
and the vulnerable are exploited and abused;

where war breeds cruelty and torture
and leaves hunger and homelessness in its wake:
> **God our hope and our deliverer,**
> **shatter the rod of violence**
> **and let your light bring peace to our darkness.**

Jan Berry

Make Us Aware

Merciful God, forgive
> that we fall asleep
> when you call us to watch and pray.
> **We fail to see the signs of your coming.**

Christ our Saviour, forgive
> that we are not watchful
> we do not choose hope
> or plant the seeds of hopefulness.
> **We fail to see the signs of your coming.**

Forgiving Spirit, forgive
> that in the rush of the Christmas season
> we forget to stop and listen for the sound of angel
>   voices
> we forget to stop and look for a star
> to guide us to Christ.
> **We fail to see the signs of God's presence.**

> God over all
> Christ within us
> Spirit around us
> hear our prayer
> and send your messenger
> of peace to us and to your sleeping world.

Kate McIlhagga

Yes, God: Let It Be

In our hope for the long-awaited liberation
in our dream of empowering the poor
in the exultation of anger and the cry of freedom
joyfully we sing out:
Yes, God: let it be.

When our destiny is caught up in God's hand
and the mystery of purpose overshadows our planning;
when we shrink from knowing ourselves part of the promise
fearfully we whisper:
Yes, God: let it be.

In the struggle we sought to avoid
in the ridicule we feared to encounter
in the pain we hoped we would never have to bear
reluctantly we cry out:
Yes, God: let it be.

To the unknown future where dreams dance and disappear
where tyranny rages, struts and falls in disgrace;
to the risk which is the price of our freedom
defiantly we shout out:
Yes, God: let it be.

Jan Berry

Come Humbly, Holy Child

Come humbly, holy child,
Stir in the womb
Of our complacency;
Shepherd our vision
Of the little we need
For abundant living.

Come humbly, holy spirit,
To whisper through the leaves
In the garden of our ignorance,
Exposing our blindness
to children dying,
Hungry and in pain.
　　Come humbly, holy light,
Pierce our lack of generosity and love,
Scattering our dark fear
Of living freely in your way,
Poured out in wanton service.
　　Come humbly, holy wisdom,
Cry through the empty street
Of our pretence to care,
That the face of the poor
Will be lifted up,
For holy is your name
　　Come humbly, holy God,
Be born into our rejoicing,
Come quickly, humble God,
And reign.

G. K. from a Mothers' Union Day on the Magnificat

Come to Us, Lord Jesus Christ

Come to us, Lord Jesus Christ,
come as we search the Scriptures and see God's hidden
　purpose,
come as we walk the lonely road, needing a companion,
come when life mystifies and perplexes us,
come into our disappointments and unease,
come at table where we share our food and hopes,
and, coming, open our eyes to recognise you.

Donald Hilton

Come, Lord Jesus

Leader: In our watching and our waiting
All: **Come, Lord Jesus**
Leader: In our hopes and in our fears
All: **Come, Lord Jesus**
Leader: In our homes and in our world
All: **Come, Lord Jesus**
Leader: Come, Lord Jesus. Bless us and surprise us
as we look forward to your birthday.
All: **Amen**

Christian Aid

Wachet Auf

After hearing Chorale Prelude by Bach

Advent
Season when
Dual citizenship
Holds us in
Awkward tension.

The world, intent on
Spending Christmas,
Eats and drinks its way to
Oblivion after dinner.

The Kingdom sounds
Insistent warnings:
Repent, be ready,
Keep awake
He comes.

Like some great fugue
The themes entwine:
The Christmas carols
Demanding our attention

In shops and pubs,
Bore their insistent way
Through noise of traffic;
Underneath, almost unheard,
The steady solemn theme of
Advent.

With growing complexity,
Clashing, bending,
Rivals for our attention,
Themes mingle and separate,
Pulling us with increasing
Urgency,
Until in final resolution,
The end attained,
Harmony rests in aweful
Stillness, and
The child is born.

He comes,
Both Child and Judge.

And will he find us
Watching?

Ann Lewin

Circles of Grace

Holy One:
We live at mystery's edge,
Watching for a startling luminescence
Or a word to guide us.

In fragile occurrences
You present yourself
And we must pause to meet you.

Daily, there are glimmers,
Reflections of a seamless mercy
Revealed in common intricacies.

These circles of grace
Spill out around us
And announce that we are a part of you.

Keri Wehlander
Canada

Winter Waiting

Last leaves drift down now,
Trees standing bare along the skyline –
Each branch etched clear against the winter light.
On the dark fields the furrows turn
To bare-backed ridges whitened hard by frost.
Yet deep within this sullen soil
New life already waits for birth –
Release to life by the returning spring.

Regenerating God, harrow our hearts
Till we become the opened ground
In which your Spirit's seeds
Take root and grow.

Jill Jenkins

The Ready Song

Lord make me ready to hear
                    ready to see
                    ready to receive your gift of love
                    ready to do
                    ready to go
                    ready for all you're making ready for me.

Lord make me ready to hear your story
        ready to see your glory
        ready to receive your gift of love – that's Jesus!
        ready to do what's right
        ready to go spread your light
        ready for all you're making ready for me.

Lord make me ready to hear that wonderful story
        ready to see you're the King of glory
ready to receive your gift of love – hallelujah, that's Jesus!
        ready to do what you show me is right and
        ready to go spread the gospel light and
        ready for all you're making ready for me.

Jenny Dann

To Wish You Well

Lights are lit,
Candles glow,
Advent trees already twinkle
Silently – bearing gifts –
Awaiting their moment,
In each window – reflecting,
Presently poised;
Lovingly wrapped
To wish you well.

So, spare time
To dream;
To admire.

In the stature of waiting,
In the magic of wondering –
Christmas mysteries unfold.
Today, every day,
So precious, so priceless;

Soon to be with us anew;
Prepare then the holly bough
And ringing bell
To welcome God, Emmanuel.

Wendy Whitehead

Journeying with Mary

Conception

Her tears conceived this child,
      as she laid her soul bare to God.
The holy man thought she was drunk,
        but he was wrong and out of touch.

   'Samuel, my child,' said Hannah.

The holy Spirit conceived this child,
      which grew with life within her womb.
She never let a man come near, until
      her labour days were passed.

   'Jesus, my child,' said Mary.

A man and a woman conceived this child,
      in wedlock but without parental love.
The child survived in life, searching
    for a heart of love.

   'My Beloved Child,' said Jesus.

Frances Ballantyne

What Child is This?

Joseph Reflects on the Annunciation

'An angel came to me', she said;
Glimmer of glory in the wrap of wings.
Greeting her gladly, with strange salutation,

That she, a virgin still, should bear a son.
'The Son of God', she said.
What fantasy is this?
She is to be my wife – my cherished ornament
Close to my heart in love and honour bound.
What shame must sound from such a revelation –
Two families disgraced – the pain of pride – the
bitterness of loss.
What can I say of her – that she is mad?
That witless she may wander through the world –
Yet, witless, innocence may still be hers?
How can I turn against my beloved
Whose brightness lies so breathless on my heart?
How can I brand her whore
Whose hand is in my hand while life may last?
What mystery is this,
That she who is my wife, within her womb,
Carries creation's child, and brings to birth
The promises of God?
I cannot understand what work is here –
Yet, as my fingers fashion at my trade,
I trust that all is well – I feel the tools strike true,
And in the fall of shavings glimpse a drift of wings.

Jill Jenkins

Mary's Lament

Who am I
That, chosen, I should travel now in pain
Through darkness?
That I should ride
Upon a simple beast
Along the journey of my travail,
Not knowing when or where
My lying in shall be?

It is cold,
Cold and bleak upon the way –
And my exhausted body
Seeks some other comfort now,
But there is none
And no escaping this.
The final culmination of my time.

Who is this babe
That he should rack me so
With pain upon His coming?
And no rest, no rest
To succour me on His arrival.
He comes with endless hardship . . .

But my child is all my hope –
To me a simple child
Who waits dependently upon my sustenance
For nourishment by body and by love.

So why this fear for him?
Who is he then?
And why, why me
To bring him forth?

I wonder, will the world be kind to him?

The mother in me fears
Some strange pre-sentiment of doom
For him, my unborn son –
That endlessly the world unleashes
Venom on the innocent,
And tears them limb from limb
On small excuse . . . or none.

What have I done
To carry such a burden

In the hollow of my heart?
How can I keep him safe
Knowing as I do

My love can offer scant protection
From his fate?

How can I keep Him safe?

I cannot.

Margot Arthurton

Expectation

My soul magnifies the Lord
and I dance with God who liberates me,
for she has remembered with love
                the whispered song of her shadow.
Surely, from now on my story will be
                handed down to all generations.
For the One who is Love
                has cradled my life in her arms
        and beautiful is her name.
Her tenderness enfolds our brokenness
            through all generations.

Her voice clamours in shouts of justice,
wrenching free the grip of the abuser.
She gathers the abused to her breast,
                her milk nurturing those who seek her,
                according to the promise given to
                our grandmothers,
                to Sarah and Hagar
                    and their children for ever.

Clare McBeath

Blessing is Not To Be Taken Lightly

Of all women you are the most blessed (Luke 1:42)

The time of worship draws to a close
and we prepare to return to the world
with a final blessing,
a 'wrap around' source of comfort,
a defence against unknown ills –
>'The blessing of God Almighty,
>Father, Son and Holy Spirit
>Go with you and remain with you . . .'

We go out strengthened, reassured,
God is with us.

And yet it can be a fearful thing
to be singled out for blessing.
To be blessed above all women meant for Mary
>a child conceived before marriage;
>giving birth to that child in an outhouse,
>watching that same child grow
>>to strike out on a course of life
>>which could threaten the whole family
>and then to see him crucified.

But not only Mary,
Saints and martyrs are regarded as greatly blessed,
but they hardly have peaceful lives.

> **Lord, we need your blessing**
> **to make us whole, fulfilled people;**
> **but if that blessing should lead us**
> **into strange and difficult paths**
> **we ask that you will strengthen**
> **our faith and our trust**
> **that we may accept what you would do with us**
> **so that blessed,**
> **we may in turn be blessing to others.**

Edmund Banyard

31

Mary of Nazareth

Hail Mary, woman of Nazareth,
home maker, cleaner, preparer of food, fetcher of water,
God is with you
in your everyday excursions in this ordinary town.
Blessed are you among women
and blessed indeed are women
in their everyday lives,
in the confines of family life,
in the ambivalence of decision making,
in the silences
and blessed are the fruits of all our labours.

Janet Lees

Announcing

Lover of my soul,
I give you thanks for Mary,
obedient, expectant, surprised and ecstatic.
For her patient waiting, her quiet questioning,
her readiness to receive, her willingness to give,
for her magnificent song of praise
and the welcoming womb for Jesus.

Holy Redeemer,
we rejoice that you tumble the proud
and lift up the humble;
that you send the rich away with nothing
and pour out blessings for the poorest of the poor.
We give you thanks
that you call out your chosen nation
and you give your blessing to all nations.
You have done great things for all people;
you never cease to give us cause for joy.

God of time and eternity,
we are thankful that you speak to your people
through angelic messengers,
through dreams and visions.
Help us to put aside hesitations and doubts;
deliver us from half-heartedness.
May we respond to your call
with heart and soul and abundant offerings.

In the beginning your word created
and there was light and life.
In the fulness of time
you sent your Word amongst us,
the Word assumed flesh and was alongside us.
Your Word brought that light;
the light shines still in the darkness
and the darkness will never extinguish the light.

John Johansen-Berg

Preparing to Celebrate

Advent in the Convent

It is Advent;
you can hear the joy
in sandalled feet,
hurrying to the chapel.

It is Advent;
and there's expectation
in the rising song,
rising and swelling,
like great waves breaking on a distant shore.

It is Advent;
full of promise
as the apple trees in Spring
and the happy smile of a young mother;
when candles burn brighter
and there's a strange thrill
in the winter song of the birds.

It is Advent;
a glorious time
to die with Christ and be hid with God
in Him,
waiting for Spring;
rising again like the song
of the skylark.

It is Advent;
breaks the glory

like oil overflowing from the cruse
as you rise from the ground
and lift your eyes to see
a cradle
and beyond a cross
and rank on rank of angels
to the golden throne,
where trumpet echoes trumpet,
as Christ claims you
for his own.

John Johansen-Berg

As With Madness

As with madness we prepare
For this festive time of year,
As we rush and count the days,
Advent passes in a haze,
So may our feet take us to
Places where we will meet you.

As with madness we collapse
In our armchairs to have naps,
As we eat too much and then
Fill our plates right up again,
So may we enjoy this feast,
Prompted now to share, at least.

As with madness we keep on
Trying to ignore your Son,
Timely God now takes a risk,
Bawling babe now shakes a fist,
So may each of us now see
Christ has come to set us free.

Tune: Dix

Janet Lees

35

Christmas Rush

Ready for Christmas?
You're joking!
With all
I've got to do,
I'll be lucky if
I'm ready by
This time next year.

Stir-up Sunday
Found me without even
The ingredients,
Let alone the time to
Stir them . . .

The cards –
I was going to write
More than
'Hope all is well'
This year
But I haven't . . .

Shopping's a nightmare,
With all those people
Intent on spending
Christmas . . .

Working out who's
Visiting who, and
Who'll be offended
If we don't . . .

The tree, the decorations,
Enough food for the cat,
Not to mention us,
I'll never be ready.

But I'm certainly ready for
Christmas – that moment when
The world seems hushed
In silent expectation,
The light in the stable
Draws us from chaos
To the stillness of
God at the centre,
And love is born.

I'm longing for that.

Ann Lewin

Question

I run a large shopping mall and with that goes all the attendant Christmas glitz, grottoes, trees, decorations, sales figures. I also inherited a tradition of the local churches coming together for a small service of readings and carols on Christmas Eve. This has varied from the small and almost unnoticed to the organised and advertised when, one year, our local radio station used us a venue.

One year the owners of the Centre declared that carol services were out. Personal preference perhaps but they were considered outmoded and not suitable. The year progressed and as we went through Autumn and published our Christmas schedule of events, children's entertainment, discount evenings and the like, there was, obviously, no carol service mentioned.

The calls then began and the visits to my office. 'Why?' shaped in all forms and from all kinds of people, 'why was there to be no service?'

And I, in turn, asked 'why?', 'why did they want a service?' They had supermarkets and baubles, they had alcohol and turkey stuffing, why did they want a service when they probably wouldn't even attend?

And the answer haunts me . . . 'I don't go to church, I wouldn't go to church . . . but I want to be reminded that there is a meaning, somewhere . . . and that someone will be there to remind me, even if I still ignore it. And if the only place I visit during this season is a shopping mall then that is where Christ must be.'

We had, and continue to have our service . . . and I remain haunted.

Wendy White

A Voice from Honduras

On one Orthodox Christmas Eve (6 January) I visited the Church of the Nativity in Bethlehem along with a group who had come especially for the consecration of Bishop Riah Abu El-Assal as the new Anglican Bishop of Jerusalem. Amongst that group was Bishop Leo Frade and his wife Diana from Honduras. Bishop Leo is the Episcopal Bishop of Honduras and his is the fastest growing Episcopal Church in the Americas. They suffered tremendously under the impact of Hurricane Mitch but they are now rebuilding their lives and community. I asked him whether there was anything special that they did at Christmas to prepare for the coming of Jesus and he told me about la Posada. This is a custom which happens in Honduras in the Episcopal (Anglican) or Catholic Churches – it is part of the Spanish tradition and it is done throughout Latin America.

The Posada means 'shelter' or 'inn' and people prepare for Christmas in the seven days before by visiting houses and singing outside them with special Christmas carols. It is to remind people of when Joseph and Mary came looking for a place to stay. However, Leo and Diana pointed out that it's different from carol singing in the States or in Europe because the people in the house deny you entry so you keep on singing and they keep saying 'There's no room, there's no room.' It's done several times and finally they will say, 'Come in' and then there's more singing inside and they offer you coffee and cookies. The songs are special ones that relate to the journey of Mary and Joseph and they talk of their travel and how they are weary and looking for a place to stay. Every night people go out to a different place. Everything has to be planned beforehand because, as Bishop Leo points out, 'If they say "come in" straight away, you blow it! They need to deny entry several times.

'In a way it's an acted parable that is both fun and significant. Children dress up as Joseph and Mary and the whole thing speaks to the community and to many who don't come to church.'

Bishop Leo says that the message of this and the message of Advent that we are communicating is, 'Let's make sure we have room for Jesus – get ready for Jesus and make sure when he knocks on our door, we have room for him.'

Another custom in Honduras is the creation of cribs. During Advent people go from house to house to see the different cribs. In the cathedral, half the church becomes a nativity scene and it's a combination of the modern with the old. There will be extra figures there, maybe soldiers or ladies making tortillas – they buy clay models. Then on the corner there will be the traditional scene of Mary and Joseph, animals and shepherds. The display is so big that it's like a city; indeed, it's modelled on the city of San Pedro Sulka where Bishop Leo and Diana live and there are even streets and cars and bridges and running water. It's fun and a community event for everyone and everyone brings different pieces.

Their homes are also turned into cribs and both in the homes and in the cathedral there are three kings and a camel who start from far away on Christmas Day and gradually start to come closer until 6 January. There is also a tradition of stealing the baby Jesus from the crib. This is the Orthodox influence reminding people that Christmas should be celebrated on 6 January and so you may lose the baby from your crib scene but the baby will re-emerge on 6 January!

Although it's now changing, Christmas Day was not the gift time in Honduras – it was 6 January, to remember when the three kings brought their gifts. That's still the case, though these days it tends to be money and sweets that are put in the stocking on 6 January because the Santa Claus tradition has come down strongly from the States and so children want some presents at Christmas! But when Leo was growing up they would wait until Epiphany for their gifts.

Garth Hewitt

Las Posadas is the time to open the doors of our hearts to give shelter. How do we give shelter to Jesus? By the doing of good works. It is the preparation time for the doing and the prac- tising of the virtues. It is a time of coming together with our neighbours. It is the occasion for gathering with our families and with those who live near us.

Fiestas Navideanas

Posada prayer

Divine and Eternal Word, who descended from the Father into the heart of the virgin Mary, your love for humankind leads you to Bethlehem where you were born at midnight into a poor and humble stable. In truth, thousands of angels accompany you on this journey, and yet we, whom you came to save and lead to that Bethlehem of eternal joy, stubbornly turn away from you. Forgive us, God and Lord of the Universe and help us to walk alongside Mary and Joseph thus giving us the courage to fight against and triumph over every adversity. **Amen.**

'Divino', the Mexican American Cultural Centre,
San Antonio, 1981

How Long Does It Take to Make an Angel?

That's the question Sarah Ernacio of the Barcelona Multi- Purpose Co-op in the Philippines was asked when she visited the headquarters of Traidcraft, the Christian based fair trade organisation.

Providing the abaca fibre for these small Christmas decorations is cut, and wire wings made up, then four angels can be made in a day. Sarah explained how making them has transformed the lives of local families.

'The families who make the angels know that their work is appreciated because of the numbers that the buyers order. In their minds they are thinking, these people on the other side of the globe really appreciate this craft that we are making. They are lifted up by that. It gives them self-esteem.

'The families who make the angels have a different outlook on life. They have a different direction now and a value of knowing what it is to have a bit of money for medicine and basic needs.'

Sarah helped to start the co-op and the child centre programme which helps with feeding, kindergarten, schooling and Christian education. Hand in hand with schooling for the children is skills training for the parents, so that the child centre and the co-op are making a real contribution to the local community.

Before Sarah returned home she shared this wish. 'We wish our angels could fly to you!' she said. 'If these angels could fly we wouldn't have the cost of transporting them!'

Fiona Ritchie Walker
Traidcraft

A Giving Time

Advent is a twinkling time
Of stars and candles
Of bright Christmas lights in city streets.
Advent is a time of light,
To celebrate the light
That Jesus brought.

Christmas is a giving time
Of presents and cards,
Of mince pie parties and shared Christmas lunch.

Christmas is a time of gifts
To celebrate the gift
That Jesus brought.

This twinkling, giving time
Is full of promise, expectation, hope
As we celebrate the big surprise:
God's greatest gift – The Christ.
But do we look for new surprises?
Do we look for God
Amongst our gifts and Christmas lights?

Virginia Becher

Christmas Magic

I want a magical Christmas –
the glow of firelight and candles,
carols, almost tuneful, on the night air,
snow beginning to fall on Christmas eve,
softly turning the world to white.

I want a magical Christmas –
cards and holly and gaudy decorations,

with their extravagance of colour,
small surprises, brightly wrapped,
and tree lights cheering the dark windows.

I want a magical Christmas –
hidden preparation of secrets,
and the busy fun of shared baking,
the joy of anticipation,
waiting for unknown delights.

I want a magical Christmas –
the re-capturing of a tender, fairy-tale world,

made vulnerable by our harsh realities,
but speaking still of innocence and trust,
and hope.

Jan Berry

Celebration in El Salvador

Two aid workers were living in a village in El Salvador.

When it came to December they asked the family at the house where they ate what happened at Christmas, 'We kill a pig and eat it,' said Reina, the mother. 'Good', said the two aid workers, because they wanted a change from eating beans and tortillas three times a day every day.

On Christmas morning they went to Reina's house looking forward to a good meal. They were given the famous and much talked about Christmas tamales. Tamales are maize cakes wrapped in a banana leaf with a tiny piece of pig bone in each one. Reina had killed the pig and the family had made five hundred tamales – enough for everyone in the village.

Apart from that the day was little different from any other day of the year. The men went to the fields and the women washed clothes in the river.

The only other thing about Christmas is that the priest would come and have a special Mass. All through the evening men and children would let off firecrackers so the service was interspersed with huge bangs. At one stage in the service the catechists let off a big roman candle behind the altar so the priest giving the homily was lit up by the light of the firework colours.

Christian Aid
Scotland

43

Advent Worship

Advent Songs

Advent Candle Song

Come and light the candles on the Advent ring
scattering the darkness till the world shall sing.

We are all God's people, waiting in this place.
hoping that in Jesus we shall see God's face.

Prophet voices speaking clear, like a burning flame,
making sure our world will never be the same.

John the Baptist telling us God wants to forgive,
calling us to change the way we work and live.

Mary, full of courage, echoing God's yes,
going on the journey God will greatly bless.

Jesus in the midst of us, filling us with joy,
giving us the life which nothing can destroy.

Tune: Glenfinlas

Christian Aid

Prepare the Way of God

Each valley shall be lifted up
and every mountain and hill made low (Isaiah 40:4)

Prepare the way of God!
Make straight the royal way.
A choir of voices shall proclaim
The advent of God's day.

Each valley shall be filled,
And hill and mount made low.
The crooked places shall be straight,
And smooth the roughest road.

A single voice shall cry
Upon the Jordan's shore
And speak the words that bring new life
To us, for evermore.

Prepare the way of God!
Make straight the royal way.
A choir of voices shall proclaim
The advent of God's day.

Tune: St Thomas

Michael Jacob Kooiman
Canada

Sarah's God

The God of Sarah praise
who turned her grief to joy
when, after many barren days,
she held her boy.

45

For laughter out of tears,
and bitterness and strife,
she praised God, after ninety years,
for the gift of life.

The God of Miriam praise!
She saw her brother found,
and learned, like him, that all God's earth
is holy ground.
When Moses sang a psalm,
'God has triumphed gloriously!'
She led the girls in song and dance
across the sea.

Praise to the God of Ruth,
a widowed refugee.
She pledged her word and kept her troth
to Naomi.
Praise God for loyalties,
kind hearts and saving hands,
and God protect all families
in foreign lands.

All praise to Mary's God
who overcame her dread.
'Behold the handmaid of the Lord.
Amen!' she said.
She sang, 'My soul, adore
God who brought down mighty kings,
and fills the hungry and the poor
with all good things.'

The matriarchs' God and ours
who leads us onward still,
inspire our hearts, unite our minds
to work God's will.

Rock, Saviour, Maker, Lamb,
we sing your praise anew.
Mother, Father, great 'I am',
we worship you.

Tune: Leoni

Barbara Moss

Candle Meditations

Advent Candles

Week 1

We light this candle
> to recall prophetic voices
> which announced the Prince of peace,
> which foretold the age of gold,
> which called for justice
> and announced the song of happiness.
> May the light overcome the darkness.

Week 2

We light this candle
> to recall the shepherds on the hills
> and all throughout the ages
> who in their place of work
> have been ready to hear good news
> and delighted to pass it on to others.
> May the light overcome the darkness.

Week 3

We light this candle
> to recall Simeon and Anna
> and all those who are the Quiet in the Land
> who have awaited every generation
> for the glory of the Lord to be revealed
> and have patiently accepted your will and timing.
> May the light overcome the darkness.

Week 4

We light this candle
    to recall Mary and Joseph
    who saw their visions and dreamed their dreams,
    who heard angelic announcements
    and were obedient to your word and their calling,
    giving a home and care to the child.
    May the light overcome the darkness.

Christmas Day

We light this candle
    for the baby of Bethlehem,
    for the child born to be king,
    for the boy in the cradle
    who became the man on the cross,
    the Redeemer and Saviour of the world.
    The darkness is overcome; the light is around us.

John Johansen-Berg

Sources of Light

*Each candle is a symbol of a different source of God – created
light, which reflects the never-failing presence of God. We thank
God and pray for ourselves and our brothers and sisters in his
world.*

Advent 1

Voice 1

Spontaneous sun
generous giver of light
heat and energy   *Light first candle*

49

Voice 2

    Father God
    we thank you for the sun
    for its rising and setting
    that never fails.
    We pray for all your people
    in the daytime,
    be with those in work
    be with those out of work,
    help us not to waste these hours of light
    Amen

Advent 2

Voice 1

    Mysterious moon
    silver crescent, milky sphere
    reflecting, changing   *Light second candle*

Voice 2

    Mother God
    we thank you for the moon
    for its waxing and waning
    that never fails.
    We pray for all your people
    in the night-time,
    be with those who sleep
    be with those who are awake,
    help us to be refreshed
    by the hours of darkness.
    Amen

Advent 3

Voice 1

    Stars without number
    gathered in forms and patterns
    that shine together   *Light third candle*

Voice 2

Father and Mother God,
thank you for the stars and the planets
for their light and shapes
that never fail.
We pray for all your people
that we may learn to live together,
to love each other
to work together
to make your world a better place.
Amen

Advent 4

Voice 1

Orange flame burning
fire, breathing, consuming,
refining our thoughts   *Light fourth candle*

Voice 2

Holy Spirit three in one
we thank you for the flame
symbol of your presence
that never fails.
We pray for all your people
that we may keep your Advent flame
alight in our lives,
help us not to extinguish it
when Christmas is past.
Amen

Christmas Day

Voice 1

Christ, light of the world
growing from creation's birth
source of life and hope   *Light fifth candle*

Voice 2

      Jesus, Lord and Saviour
      we thank you for this day of celebration
      the renewal of your love for us
      that never fails.
      We pray for all your people
      that today even in the darkest corners
      your lamp may be lit
      and your light may shine
      giving joy and peace.
      Amen

Heather Johnston

Reflections by Candlelight

This act of collective worship was conducted on a first Monday of Advent at Holy Trinity Church of England Aided School, Stockton on Tees. Worship explores the truth that despite outward differences we are all capable of allowing God to shine through us. As Jesus is the light of the world for Christians, we can also be lights of comfort, guidance and goodness to other people.

As children enter:

Play a recording of 'Shepherd Moons' by Enya.

An Advent candle is lit at the commencement of worship. A student lights the candle from a taper.

Leader: The Lord be with you.

All: **And also with you.**

Prayer: Thank you for the candle
           that we light on a morning
      Thank you for our cross
           that helps us to think about God

52

Thank you for being Lord of the World
For love, peace and joy.

Hymn: reflecting the theme of 'Light'

The leader produces a large shopping carrier and invites the children to go forward and put a hand in the bag where they find a variety of coloured, differently shaped candles.

Talk with the children about the different colours and shapes. Then using a taper light each candle. The meeting place will become brighter, eyes will widen. Draw out from the children that each candle gives the same light regardless of colour or shape. We can all shine for God in our communities. Talk about what this can mean. Make sure the candles are safely on the floor or a table. Hold hands to show our unity and respect for each other.

Hymn: If possible, sing 'Flickering Candles' or 'See All the Candles'.

As an aid for getting ready for Christmas show winter scenes/shopping scenes on an overhead projector or other media means. Then, one by one extinguish the candles leaving only the Advent Candle burning brightly. Extinguish it with a snuffer and leave the smoke to curl upwards, explaining that the candle will be lit at the next time of worship as we continue to approach Christmas.

Close with the Blessing.

All: **Go in peace to love and serve the Lord**
             In the Name of Christ. Amen

Play again quietly 'Shepherd Moons' by Enya.

Adapted from an article by Dave Bellett

Responsive Prayers for Lighting the Advent Candles

Advent Sunday

The first candle is lit.

Leader: One candle in the darkness and the dark is filled with light. God is light and our lives are judges in the light of God's love. God is love and we look forward to the time when God's will is done and the Kingdom will come.

Reader: The people who walked in darkness have seen a great light; light has dawned on them, living in a land as dark as death.

Prayer: God of all hope, fill us with joy and peace; we trust you. We pray that in the darkness of our times we may still be full of hope, looking for the coming of Christ in our world. The Lord hears our prayer.

All: **Thanks be to God. Amen**

Advent 2

Two candles are lit.

Leader: One candle in the darkness brings hope; the second is to remind us of the prophets who believed in God during dark days and looked forward to the coming of God's chosen one.

Reader: See, your God comes; then shall the eyes of the blind be opened and the ears of the deaf be unstopped. Then shall the lame leap for joy and the tongue of the dumb shall shout aloud!

Prayer: God of promise, we thank you for those who, since time began, have trusted your word. Let us be ready to see you, listening for your good news so that we may dance and sing our way into the Kingdom. The Lord hears our prayer.

All: **Thanks be to God. Amen**

Advent 3

Three candles are lit.

Leader: One candle for hope; the second candle for the prophets; the third candle is to tell of John the Baptist who called people to change their way of living so as to prepare for the coming of Christ.

Reader: The light shines on in the dark and the darkness has not put it out. There appeared a man named John, sent from God: he came as a witness to tell of the Light so that all might believe through him.

Prayer: God of the poor in spirit, we thank you for John the Baptist and for his call to us to turn round so that we can walk in your way. Make us faithful in waiting and ready for your coming so that we may make ready the way for Jesus to come into our lives. The Lord hears our prayer.

All: **Thanks be to God. Amen**

Advent 4

Four candles are lit.

Leader: One candle in the darkness for hope; the second for the prophets; the third for John the Baptist. The fourth is for Mary who simply and gladly responded to the call of God.

Reader: 'Here am I', said Mary, 'I am the Lord's servant. As you have spoken, so be it.'

Prayer: God of the humble, we thank you for choosing Mary and for her readiness and joy in answer to your call. Help us to understand the way of the lowly and to share in the humility through which Christ may be born even in a stable, even in our hearts. The Lord hears our prayer.

All: **Thanks be to God. Amen**

Norwyn Denny

An Advent Candle Ceremony

Advent Sunday
All God's People Waiting in Hope

Leader: The Lord God will wipe away all tears from all faces, and it will be said on that day, 'Lo, this is our god; we have waited for him, that he might save us. Let us be glad and rejoice in his salvation.' (Isaiah 25:8, 9)

We light the first candle on our Advent Ring to celebrate how all God's people around the world are watching and waiting for the promises of God to come true. Every year we look forward to Christmas because of the life and the hope that it promises. Every year we realise that peace has not yet come to earth and that the suffering of the poor has not ended. We celebrate because, along with many others, we are people who refuse to give up hope – and that kind of hope is stronger than anything else in the world.

Advent Candle Song (to be found on page 44)

> *Sing the first two verses during which the candle is lit.*

Leader: With those who are poor
All: **We believe in life before death.**

Leader: With those whom nobody notices
All: **We believe in life before death.**

Leader: With those who have nowhere to lay their head
All: **We believe in life before death.**

Leader: With those who can't rely on government,
or armies,
or the world community to help them
All: **We believe in life before death.**

Leader: Because you, O God, came among us as one of these
All: **We believe in life before death.**

Leader: As for us, we have this large crowd of witnesses
round us. So then, let us rid ourselves of everything
that gets in the way and of the sin that holds onto us
so tightly and let us keep our eyes fixed on Jesus, on
whom our faith depends from beginning to end.
(Hebrews 12:1–2a)

Prayers To be written from community and global situations
known to the congregation.

> *A globe should be placed on the altar or a table. Arrange
> for various people to bring lighted night-lights, one for
> each bidding, to surround it. Or, put night-lights around
> the globe and provide a taper for people to light them.*

Leader: All over the world, people are waiting and hoping for God's coming. They are waiting and hoping for a world where everyone will have life before death. We remember some of them today and light candles to show that we want to stand by them.

The night-lights are lit.

Leader: In our watching and our waiting
All: **Come, Lord Jesus**
Leader: In our hopes and in our fears
All: **Come, Lord Jesus**
Leader; In our homes and in our world
All: **Come, Lord Jesus**
Leader: Come, Lord Jesus. Bless us and surprise us, as we look forward to your birthday.

All: **Amen**

Advent Two
Prophets – Candles in the Darkness

Leader: The people who walked in darkness have seen a great light. They lived in a land of shadow but no light is shining on them. (Isaiah 9:2)

Today, the second Sunday in Advent, we light two candles on the Advent Ring to remind us of the prophets. The prophets of the Old Testament seem a bit strange to us. Some people think they predicted the future. Some think they just went around spreading gloom and condemning everybody. But what we celebrate about prophets is this:

- they told the truth about what was really going on in the world and they stood up for people who were poor;

58

- they believed in God's promises of life before death even when things seemed hopeless;

- they said what they thought even when they were afraid.

There are people like that in the world today as well and we celebrate them too.

Advent Candle Song (to be found on page 44)

> *Sing the first three verses during which two candles are lit.*

Leader: In the beginning when it was very dark
God said, 'Let there be light.'
All: **And there was light.**

Leader: God's light goes on shining in the darkness
All: **And the darkness has never put it out.**

Leader: Jesus said, 'You are like light for the whole world. A city built on a hill cannot be hidden. No-one lights a lamp and puts it under a bowl, instead he puts it on the lamp-stand, where it gives light to everyone in the house. (Matthew 5:14–15)

Prayers Write your own biddings and include concerns in the news.

Leader: Let us pray for those people who are going through
dark times,
a time of trouble,
a time when it is not clear what to do,
especially . . . *(name circumstances known to your congregation)*
God, in your mercy,
All: **Hear our prayer.**

Leader: Let us thank God for those people whose courage
and hope
have lit up the dark places of this world,
especially . . .
God, in your mercy,

All: **Hear our prayer.**

Leader: We pray for ourselves, that God will give us the
courage
to see things clearly and tell the truth . . .
God, in your mercy,

All: **Hear our prayer.**

Leader: The light of God to make us unafraid
The power of God to protect us
The joy of God to heal us
The grace of God to bless us and keep us truthful
now and for evermore

All: **Amen**

Advent Three
John the Baptist – Time to Change

Leader: The word of God came to John, son of Zechariah,
in the desert. So John went throughout the whole
territory of the river Jordan preaching, 'Turn away
from your sins and be baptised and God will forgive
your sins.' In many different ways John preached
the good news to the people and urged them to
change their ways. (Luke 3:2–3, 18)

Today, the third Sunday in Advent, we light three
candles to remind us of John the Baptist. He told
people that Jesus was coming but that meant things
would have to change. He said that we should make
the world a fairer place for poor people who don't
have enough to eat and who get treated badly by

60

people with more power. Life is still very unfair for lots of people and it doesn't help if we all think nothing can ever change.

Advent Candle Song (to be found on page 44)

> *Sing verses one to four during which three candles are lit.*

Leader: O God, we live in a world that needs to change. We are part of that world and we do things or let things happen that hurt other people.
We say to God:

All: **O God, help us to change our ways.**

Leader: O God, we live in a world which pretends that nothing can ever really change and that things can never be fair. But you have promised a different world which is good news for the poor.
We say to God:

All: **O God, help us to change our ways.**

Leader: Listen to God's words, words for those who want to change. In Jesus, God says to us:
'Come with me, your sins are forgiven. Don't be afraid.'

Prayers:

Leader: Let us pray for homes where things are changing:

where there is a new baby
where someone has left home or is moving house
where someone is ill or someone has died
where someone has lost their job or has a new job

where people are considering a change in their lives
God, in your mercy,

All: **Hear our prayer.**

Leader: Let us pray for countries where things are changing:

where there is a new government and new hope or
   new fears
where prices are going up
where schools or hospitals are closing
where there is war and violence
God, in your mercy,

All: **Hear our prayer.**

Leader: Let us pray for people who make things change:

leaders who have power but don't always do good
   things with it
people who try to change the law so that it will be
   better for poor women and men
people in the media who say things that people
   listen to
ordinary people who make the world a better place
people who have changed situations whereby poor
   and marginalised people have been helped and
   given opportunities to be self-supporting.
God, in your mercy,

All: **Hear our prayer.**

Leader: As we plan and make decisions
All: **God be our way.**

Leader: As we learn and ask questions
All: **God be our truth.**

Leader: As we grow and as we change
All: **God be our life.**

Advent Four
Mary – Saying 'Yes' to the Journey

Leader: Mary said: 'My heart praises the Lord; my soul is glad because of God my Saviour, for he has remembered me, his lowly servant! From now on all people will call me happy, because of the great things the mighty God has done for me!' (Luke 1:46–9)

Today, the fourth Sunday in Advent, we light four candles to remember Mary. When she was told she was going to be the mother of Jesus she knew it would be hard because she was just a young girl.

In her life, she had some hard journeys to make;
to Bethlehem where Jesus was born
to Egypt where they had to go to escape the soldiers
and to the cross where she watched her son die.

She couldn't have known how hard it would be but she said 'yes' to God's call because it was a call to life. All over the world women still take on hardship because they want to create a life that is worth living for their children.

Advent Candle Song (to be found on page 44)

> *Sing verses one to five during which four candles are lit.*

Leader: When the world began
All: God said yes.

Leader: When Jesus came
All: God said yes.

Leader: When we were born
All: **God said yes**
God says yes to life and loving.

Leader: God calls us
All: **To enjoy loving**

Leader: God calls us
All: **To be like Mary**

Leader: God calls us
All: **To life and loving**
God, when you call us, help us to say yes.

Leader: God you created every part of me
You put me together in my mother's womb
When my bones were being formed
When I was growing there in secret
You knew that I was there –
You saw me before I was born
God where could I go to escape from you?
Where could I get away from your presence?
If I flew away beyond the East
or lived in the farthest place in the West
You would be there to lead me
You would be there to help me.

(From Psalm 139)

Prayers:

Leader: We pray for people whose journeys are hard and
dangerous . . . *(name people and situations known to
you)*
We pray for people who are afraid of what they
will find at the end of their journey
We pray for people whose journeys are happy and
hopeful . . .

64

We pray for the people who make our journeys
    possible
We pray for ourselves that we may be ready to
    go where God calls . . . *(name people who have
    responded to go to a situation where people are in
    need of help)*

All: **Hear our prayer.**

Leader: We say the blessing together:
All: **Bless to us O God the road that is before us**
    Bless to us O God the friends who are around us
    Bless to us O God your love which is within us
    Amen

Christmas Day
Christ's Birth – Giving and Receiving

Leader: Out of the fullness of his grace God has blessed us
giving us one blessing after another. (John 1:16)

Today is Christmas Day which is all about giving
people things. God loves giving us all that we need
and much more. When Jesus was born it was as if
God's love overflowed, spilling out into the world,
making our ordinary life special and giving us joy
we didn't have before. We can become part of God's
love when we give up just holding on to what we've
got, when we are happy because people give us
things and when we have fun giving things to other
people. Today, we light all the candles including the
one in the middle which stands for Jesus.

Advent Candle Song (to be found on page 44)

*Sing the six verses of the song during which time the
candles are lit.*

65

Leader: For some people, Christmas goes wrong and we
will pray for them:
for everyone who is lonely or sad today

All: **Give them your love, O God.**

Leader: For everyone who didn't get a present

All: **Give them your love, O God.**

Leader: For everyone who couldn't afford to give presents

All: **Give them your love, O God.**

Leader: For everyone who has rows instead of laughter

All: **Give them your love, O God.**

Leader: For everyone who is disappointed or jealous

All: **Give them your love, O God.**

Leader: For everyone who gets too busy or tired to have fun

All: **Give them your love, O God.**

Leader: For everyone who doesn't know how to give or
how to receive happily

All: **Give them your love, O God.**

Leader: Jesus said:
'Ask and you will receive;
Seek and you will find;
Knock and the door will be opened to you.'
(Matthew 7:7)

Prayers:

Leader: God's light goes on shining in the darkness
All: **And the darkness has never understood it.**

Leader: God's light goes on shining in the darkness
All: **And the darkness has never put it out.**

Leader: Generous God,
we do not know why you keep on giving to us
we do not understand your joy.
But give us such pleasure this Christmas
in giving to other people
and receiving from them

that we may begin to understand and become
more like you,
through Jesus Christ
All: **Amen.**

Christian Aid

Advent Prayers

Advent Prayer

Lord of all time
Bless this season,
Come amongst us
In all we do.
Help us prepare
For Your coming,
Not merely to scuttle
To and fro,
In a frenzy
Of cooking and shopping,
Parties and glitter,
Worthless waste
Of precious time
Given by You.

Lesley K. Steel
Scotland

A Litany for Advent

Leader: Holy God, this is earth's quiet season, the
season of waiting.
All: **We rest in the shelter of your love.**
Leader: This is the season of darkness, when we seek
stars to guide us.
All: **We trust in the light of your promise.**
Leader: This is the season of solitude, when we listen for
our own heart's rhythm.
All: **We find warmth in the signs of your presence.**

Leader:	This is our season to make room, a time to make ready.
All:	**For we shall join in the angels' chorus.**
Leader:	Peace on earth, goodwill to all.
All:	**Peace on earth, goodwill to all.**

Keri Wehlander
Canada

The One Who Comes

Prayers of intercession

Lord you come to bring good news for the poor.
We hold before you the poor people in our community
the ones who will not have enough to eat today
who will not have a roof over their head tonight.
We pray for all who share the struggle against poverty
charities which help to provide homes and clothes and
     money
social workers and health workers who offer support to
     individuals
politicians local and national who have to allocate
     inadequate resources.
Give to us all your loving concern for the poor at home and
     abroad
so that we will work and give and share
until the poor hear the good news of your coming.

Lord you come to bring freedom for the prisoner.
We hold before you all who will spend this day and this
     night in prison
justly or unjustly.
We pray for those for whom prison is better than the places
     they are used to
and for those who long for release.
We pray for those who administer the legal system
police and magistrates, judges and lawyers,

69

probation officers and prison officers and workers with
  Victim Support.
Give to us all a passion for justice and mercy
so that we will work and give and share
until the prisoners find freedom.

Lord you come to give recovery of sight to the blind.
We hold before you all who are visually impaired
and all who are blind because they have closed their eyes
to your love and to the pain of others.
We pray for everyone who works to bring sight to the blind
in hospitals and clinics and schools
and for those who support people whose minds are in the
  dark
through mental illness or grief or despair.
Give to us all the determination to be lights in the world
until the blind recover their sight.

Lord you come to proclaim release for the oppressed.
We hold before you all who stoop under the burden of
  oppression
for those who cannot speak freely for fear of betrayal
for those who cannot live freely because of prejudice and
  discrimination
for those whose lives have been damaged by violence and
  abuse.
We pray for workers for political freedom
for those who work for racial justice in Britain and all over
  the world.
We pray for counsellors and psychiatrists
who work to relieve the oppression of past trauma and
  restore wholeness.
Give to us all relief from the burdens we carry,
and a deep concern to bear the burdens of others,
until everywhere oppression is defeated and we are made
  whole.

Lord you come to proclaim the year of the Lord's favour.
We pray for those people who are working
for an end to the oppression of Third World debt
and release for men and women and children who are
  enslaved
working to pay back money from which they have never
  benefited
and which they can never repay.
We pray for bankers and financial decision-makers
and for ministers of state and civil servants
who have the responsibility of making the hard decisions.
Give to us all a sense of responsibility for the resources of
  the world
and for the needs of our sisters and brothers
so that we will share what we have and forgive our debtors
until the whole earth shares love's joyful Jubilee.

Through Jesus Christ our Lord
Amen

Heather Pencuvel

An Advent Eucharist

Follow the Light to Your Stable . . .

A Communion Celebration for the Advent Season and Christmas

A Communion Celebration can start either from this point or after readings, hymns and a sermon/reflection.

The Invitation:

Leader: Come, follow the light that shines for you and leads you to a stable with a manger and child.

All: **Lord, we have followed the light.**

Leader: Come, listen for the voice that calls you to find new life in the broken corners of the world.

All: **Lord, we have heard the voice.**

Leader: Come, rich and poor, neighbour or stranger, gather round and share a celebration with the Prince of Peace.

All: **Lord, we have gathered to meet with you.**

Leader: Come, like wealthy kings with priceless gifts or poor shepherds with only themselves to bring, for the Spirit has led you to this place where you are offered the promise of new life.

All: **Lord, fill us with new life.**

Narrative and Preparation:

From being a child in a manger dependent on his mother's milk for food he grew to be the Living Word made Flesh offering everyone the bread of life. He travelled from the manger to the cross where his body was broken, his love poured out but God held him like a mother and nursed him back to life.

> May we see the guiding light
> May we find you in a stable
> May we follow you to the cross
> May we find new life through you
> As we gather round the table to celebrate the beginning
>   of a journey
> from the manger to the cross and back to life again.

Jesus knew what was to come when, in that upper room, he poured water into a basin and began to wash the feet of his disciples with a towel saying 'If I do not wash your feet, you have no part with me.'

Lord, we confess that our lives and the life of the world have been broken by our sins but we come for you to wash us clean so that we may walk in new life with you.

Then, as they were eating, Jesus said: 'Truly, I say to you, one of you will betray me.' And they were sorrowful and began to ask, as we do: 'Is it I?'

May our lips not betray you, our deeds not crucify you and our love never leave you as we commit ourselves anew to walk with you.

So Jesus took bread, broke it and blessed it and asked his disciples to remember how his life was given for them and the generations to come. In the same way, after eating, he took the cup and asked them to remember how his love was poured out as a sign of a new relationship with God and for the forgiveness of sins.

Thank you for giving your life so that we may be forgiven and reconciled to God when we follow you the Risen Son. Amen

An appropriate hymn may be sung.

Thanksgiving Prayer:

O Lord, open our minds to a new understanding of your
  wonderful Word which is such a mystery but is the root of
  our faith.
Open our eyes so we can see the Spirit guiding us and open
  our hearts to share the Christ within us as we continue the
  journey of faith thanking you for all that has gone and the
  future to come:
For the faith of mothers and fathers through history
  and the sons and daughters who followed them,
For the visions of prophets and disciples
  who shared your Word and all who believed them.
For the obedience of Mary and Joseph
  called to serve you as parents of Jesus
And for the wise people and shepherds who saw a guiding
  light and heard angels sing so followed to a stable where
  they found new life in a manger.
It was the life of a child, born to be King of a Kingdom to
  come, who grew to be the man of the cross who died for
  living your Word but walked from the tomb to give us the
  hope and mystery of our faith.
So, thank you, Lord, for the Manger and the Cross and the
  journey between that gives us new hope when we walk
  with your Son.

Lord's Prayer (said or sung)

Blessing of Bread and Wine:

Holy Spirit gift of Christ, come among us and bless this bread which we take and break, remembering how Jesus gave his life for us. And Holy Spirit, gift of Christ, remain among us, and bless this cup as we remember how your love was poured out for us:

Sung Blessing:

> **Spirit of the Living God**
> **Move among us now**
> **Make us one in heart and mind**
> **Through our bread and wine:**
> **Taking, breaking,**
> **Blessing, sharing,**
> **Spirit of the Living God**
> **Bless our bread and wine.**

> *Tune: Spirit of the Living God*

Sharing of Bread and Wine:

So draw near with faith. Be strengthened by the life of our Lord Jesus Christ, who was born in a stable to be the living bread and died on a cross having poured out his love so we may drink from God's cup of forgiveness. Eat and drink. Take him into your hearts by faith with thanksgiving.

As you take bread hold it in prayer and remember how the body of Jesus was born, lived and was broken for you . . . and then we will eat together, united in the one body.
Eat together.

As you take the/a cup hold it in prayer and remember how Jesus poured out his love for you and meets your needs when he lives in your heart.
Drink together.

75

Prayer:

Thank you for bread and wine through which we have remembered your life and love and all you taught and may we now be filled with your Living Word.

> Build a stable in my body
> Place a manger in my heart
> Fill it with your love
> As if it were a new born child.
> Amen

Blessing

Richard Becher

An Advent Eucharistic Prayer

Lord God, you come to us in the simplicity of a baby,
yet are greater by far than our imagining;
Come to us, Lord.
Lord Christ, you hide your ways from the proud,
yet reveal your truth to those of a childlike spirit;
Come to us, Lord.
Lord Spirit, you overthrow the powerful,
yet empower the humble and open of heart;
Come to us, Lord.

Come to us now in your vulnerable strength,
as we remember Jesus,
who brought wholeness and life
through his death and resurrection.
On the night before he died,
he took bread and wine, blessed them
and gave them to his friends, saying,
This is my body, this is my blood,
Eat and drink to remember me.

Come freshly to us, Living God:
Bring in your Kingdom of justice and love,
Your Kingdom come;
Forgive us, that we may learn to repent,
Your Kingdom come;
Heal us, that we may be whole in your service,
Your kingdom come;
Teach us, that we may be surprised into truth,
Your Kingdom come;
For you are the God who longs to set us free
to love and serve you wholeheartedly.
Your Kingdom come in us, Lord,
and transform the world
to your praise and glory.

Ann Lewin

Advent Blessings

Advent Blessing (1)

Hold your light out to the world
   and let people of all nations
   feel the warmth of God's love
   as they encounter the Word made Flesh
   through Christ our Lord.

Follow, where the Spirit of Hope leads us
Listen, as the Child of Peace cries for us
Rejoice, as the Love of God embraces us
and let us go
with Hope, Peace and Love in our hearts
and the blessing
of Creator, Child and Spirit for ever within us.

Richard Becher

Advent Blessing (2)

Let us go in faith
to ponder in our hearts
the mystery of this moment.
And may life be born within you,
Christ Jesus be seen among you
and joy surround you like the angels' song.

Dorothy McRae-McMahon
Aotearoa New Zealand

Part Two:
Christmas

Let us go and see . . .
. . . when love comes down at Christmas

Christmas Eve

Christmas Tide

The day before Christmas Eve
an empty stable
bare, unwelcoming,
sits in an empty church.

Soon the faithful, the curious, the hopeful
will gather.
Soon the church will be filled
with warmth and praise:
soft candlelight
children's voices,
the song of the frosty stars.

And then the stable will be transformed,
filled with glory,
crowded with the Christmas cast
of donkeys and sheep,
shepherds and kings,
Mary, Joseph and the Baby,
the Holy One of Israel,
asleep on the hay.

Transform our empty spaces
O Christmas God.
Fill the empty mangers of the world
with food.
Empty the cardboard boxes,
refuge of the lonely and despairing.

Bring warmth and light and shelter
to all who watch and wait this night.

In bar and bare hillside
in barrio and back room
in crowded flat
or empty home
may we feel your presence
at our shoulder and in our hearts
and when the crib is packed away,
the figures carefully clothed
in protective covering,
unwrap the swaddling bands
unfold the truth
release the message:
an empty stable –
He's not here.
He has risen.

Kate McIlhagga

Christmas Eve

Is there room?
There rarely is
when people are desperate
and search for shelter.

Is there room?
There seldom is
when people are in danger
and beg for sanctuary.

Is there room?
There never is
when genocide is in the air
and the roads to escape are closed.

Is there room?
Will you open the door
for the child of Bethlehem,
even in the stranger's clothes?

John Johansen-Berg

No Room: We're Full

There's no room in this country,
we're full up.
In fact we're overcrowded,
there's hardly room for us
(well, for our cars, at any rate)
so we really can't take you or anyone else.
Sorry.
No really, believe me, there's no housing to spare,
none at all; especially with the rising demand
for second homes.
So you see, we really can't help you.
You must go somewhere else.
And please, move your old moke away from the Portico.
    Thanks.
The stable? What stable?
What on earth do you mean?
We couldn't put you in a stable.
This is a civilised country
and a stable, even if we had one, which we don't,
wouldn't comply with the building regulations
for human habitation.
So move away, please.

. . .

No, my dear, it's all right. They've gone now, thank God.
Just a couple of foreigners, bogus asylum seekers, probably,
in an old banger. Of course we couldn't take them in,
people like that.

Louise Pirouet

Tale of the Innkeeper

I am old, so old and weary – my eyes are growing dim
Yet I dream of the fateful evening when I had no room for
   Him.
The earth was hushed, expectant and a burning star hung low
For the Son of God's arrival but how was I to know?

When Joseph came aknocking shabby and poor
And Mary's eyes pleading, still I closed the door.
If the angels carried the message, if the heavenly host had
   said,
'The kingly child is coming,' I would have found a bed.

When I heard the angelic chorus and saw the shepherds who
   came
Gladly to kneel and worship; sick was my heart with shame;
I am old, so old and weary and this is my earnest plea
That the loving Christ of Christmas will find a place for me.

R. May Hill
Aotearoa New Zealand

The Christmas Samaritan

Poor woman!
Did you see her
   with her man?
From door to door
   they went
   a scruffy looking couple,
   wanting a place to rest:
Nothing grand,
   no evening meal,
   nor even B & B,
   just a room would do,
   with a bed to rest
   until her time was due.

Poor man!
Did you see him
  with his woman?
I saw them,
  weary from their travels,
  turned away by the priest,
  without a word of help
  and that good Christian
  from down the road
  peeped round the curtain
  saw them at the door
  so pretended she wasn't there.

Poor woman!
They found a space in a stable,
  a cold and smelly place,
  but all the man of little faith
  could offer her to rest.
'God bless you,' said the couple
but who God was
  he didn't know
  until the baby cried
  and then he found
  a new neighbour in his life
  to love with all his heart,
  body, mind and soul . . .

Richard Becher

The Light Has Come

Isaiah 60:1–6

Lord of the dawn,
where your people live in darkness
  let your light sweep in.

Lord of the noon,
where your people are dazzled by evil
let your light sweep in.

Lord of the evening,
where your people fear the night
let your light sweep in.

Lord of the night,
where your people pray for morning
let your light sweep in.

Lord of our lives,
As we grow into a new year of hopes and possibilities
let your light sweep in.

Melanie Frew

Now is the Time, the Time of God's Favour

Now is the time, the time of God's favour,
promise and hope for a people restored;
let us repent and turn back to our Saviour
truly to welcome the year of our Lord.

This is the day of Jesus' arrival;
here in the desert, the threshold of home!
After earth's longings comes heaven's revival:
God make us ready this day as you come.

Here is the hour, the hour of salvation;
learn the new song for new people to sing:
risen from death is the source of creation;
lift up your heads for the hour of the King.

Do not delay, but come now to meet him,
Sabbath and Jubilee joining in one:

Christmas and Easter and Advent will greet him;
see a fresh universe rise to the Son.

Now is the time, the time of God's favour,
promise and hope for a people restored;
let us repent and turn back to our Saviour
truly to welcome the year of our Lord.

Christopher Idle

Silent Night

Silent night
Peaceful and still
Stars out, clear sky
No wind to disturb the rest
Of those who sleep.

And yet some sounds
Faint rustle of straw
As cattle settle in stable
Soft breath of ox and ass
Chat of family and friends
Gathered in Bethlehem
Talking late into the night.

And suddenly
A piercing cry
Of mother giving birth
Cry of babe new-born
Strange on this world
Songs of angels praising
Feet running to see
The saviour of the world.

For unto us is born
This night no longer silent

The Son of God and Son of Man
Come! See and praise him.

Lesley K. Steel
Scotland

Come, Christmas God

When it's cold and wet
and we long for the light
        come Christmas.

Come to bring warmth and joy
to inn-keepers and travellers
to shepherds and kings;
Come to bring hope and peace
to refugees and security forces;
Come to comfort the lonely
and wipe the tear from the cheek
of those who are sad.

Immanuel – God with us
let your light shine
into the dark recesses
of our minds and our cities.
Let your warmth
bring forth harvests of joy.
Let your peace
enter the hearts
of those who struggle and plot
for power and advantage over others.

Come, Christmas God
Christ Child of Bethlehem
Spirit of wonder
be born in us and your world
once more

88

that joy may be shared
peace proclaimed
and love abound.

Kate McIlhagga

Crisis at Christmas

Old Tom was on a journey
and he walked on through the cold,
looking for two simple things –
a bit of grub to eat
and a middling warm place to kip.

At first he tried a house,
all lit up with coloured lights;
he rang the bell; a lady came.
'Just need a bit of food,' he said
but the door was already closed.

Next he tried a restaurant;
there's always lots of grub left over.
Knocked on the door and a bloke came out;
'Any grub, mate, you can spare?'
'Get off from here. You'll scare our customers,'
and a few spicy words as well.
Tom got the message quick and scarpered,
quick as a flash.

He thought about a church then
and pushed open the big wooden door.
He ventured in about six steps
when two men barred his way.
'You're letting in a draught,' one said
and the other 'Watch the plate'
as the sounds of the choir rose loftily
and Tom retreated, closing the old wooden door.

He decided next on another house
with a long winding path;
by now the snow was falling
and he was feeling tired and cold.
His legs would hardly carry him
and his eyes began to glaze.
He staggered across the rock-hard lawn
and with a sort of sigh, he crumpled to the ground.

It was a week later, after that heavy fall of snow,
that the thaw came and melted it
and a neighbour called the police.
Old Tom had no last supper
but he found a resting place,
a green mattress under a brown pillow for his head
and a white blanket to cover him.

John Johansen-Berg

Yesterday's News!

In the street
people rushing,
pushing and jostling
all concern for others lost,
frantically seeking the last present
thoughtlessly passing the ardent carol singers,
not even noticing the young man
selling the Big Issue.
And I wonder – what does Christmas mean?

In the world,
children crying at the sound of sirens
people looking up to the sky
fearful not of angel choirs
but the thunder of jets;
parents wondering

not at good tidings
but whether sons and daughters
will come home again
from bomber cockpits
or army barracks.
And I wonder – what does Christmas mean?

In the corridors of power,
corruption and lies
politics and partisanship
old scores settled
anger and bitterness.
And I wonder – what does Christmas mean?

And I remember:
In Bethlehem few heard angels,
they were busy with other things;
and Jesus from his birth was homeless,
and as a man he depended for shelter on others.
And I remember Herod
and recall that lies as the weapons of power,
oppression and the death of innocents
are part of the story
which we have sanitized into insignificance.

This was yesterday's news.
Here is today's news:
In this world of
selfishness and sin
of politics and pain
Christ was born.
For this world he died on a cross
and was raised.

God is with us:
In this world we have hope,
in this darkness we have light

a love which cannot die
and eternal life.

Glory to God!

Peter Trow

A Christmas Eve Thanksgiving

*On Christmas Eve in Sarajevo, during the Balkan Wars, an elderly
refugee died of hypothermia as she begged for food.*

Whisper it slowly, her name.
But do not set it in the ice mould of life's grammar –
    brown paper wrapped and empty.
(*Homo sapiens* is too measured and objective –
    a box holding what has no movement.)

Whisper it slowly, her name.
Dare to pray and half forged memories awaken –
    night's ash turns to expectancy.
(Put away conventional procedure, exact process –
    creeping reason's grip lets slip infinite echoes.)

Whisper it slowly, her name.
She is not her name, but
    grace dancing on day's fragile drift,
    a glory elevated to nuzzle eternity;
She is mysterious as yarrow and green and sky.
Whisper it slowly, her name. And you will see –
    behind the brittle convenience of naming,
    outside the edge of language,
    and the tangle of common sense –
That she is beyond naming, unrestrained, unknown.

This daze of unfamiliarity startles.
The horizon of her possibility is still.
Now she smiles on a shore which no chart can fix
And watches shearwaters glide to the sea's edge.
Pray a thanksgiving for her love to loved ones
– and for the reflexive Love of which it was a shadow.

Derek Webster

On the Eve of Christmas

(A Popular Arabic Carol)

On the Eve of Christmas	Hatred will vanish
On the Eve of Christmas	The earth will flourish
On the Eve of Christmas	War will be gone
On the Eve of Christmas	Love will be born

When we offer a glass of water to a thirsty person
it is Christmas
When we clothe a naked person with a gown of love
it is Christmas
When we wipe the tears from weeping eyes
it is Christmas

When the spirit of revenge dies in me
it is Christmas
When in my heart I no longer want to stay apart
it is Christmas
When I am buried in the being of God
it is Christmas

Sabeel Liberation Theology Centre
Jerusalem

How I'll Spend This Christmas

When Christmas Eve
ends my planning
and kids snatch sleep,
I'll push unfinished lists
from the worktop,
make some tea
and breathe again.

I hope that in the morning

I'll gaze past the glitter
of our tree, see something
of the reason behind it all.
I'll be wondering
what you're doing,
if me choosing fair trade
is working.

I want to know

your children will be smiling,
you'll find time
to hold someone's hand,
maybe think about the things
you've made,
who has them now,
how they're being used.

You won't know

my struggle, the balancing act
of buying, trying to make
the difference
when bills are large
and there are new shoes to buy.

I believe

that between us,
we'll make it.

Fiona Ritchie Walker
Traidcraft

Christmas Bells

After the Dutch of Gerrit Achterberg

Bells stroke me out of the deep pool of sleep
to tell me Christmas has come back tonight,
making its annual visit in despite
of me and the mist-web through which I creep.

It seems to batter at my door and peep
over my window-sill with that insight
some call dumb-creatures emptiness. It might
make me a saint did it not make me weep.

The town falls silent and my thinking wings
over the eaves and away to Bethlehem.
Two thousand years on, there's the stabled mother
just giving birth to the baby she will gather
up in that shawl. The coldness there with them
makes it seem sober though some drunk ass sings.

Brian Louis Pearce

Child in the Manger

Wake Up

Wake up
little baby God
thousands of children
have been born
just like you
without a roof
without bread
without protection.

A Christmas Card
Chile

We Kneel

Mary sits,

the child rocked in her womb
now rocked in her arms.

Joseph stands

the child given to him
now bound to his heart.

We kneel

the child come to us
now capturing our love.

O God come to us once more,
bind us to you
with cords of love.
Lead us with reins of kindness
and bring us to fulness of life.

Kate McIlhagga

Here at Last!

The day has come at last: it has been hard to wait
eager, sleepless, we have longed
for Christmas – to receive
presents, lovingly chosen, carefully wrapped;
people – family and friends come for the holiday
and now the day is here – it has begun!

We thank you, loving God, for the happiness of
   Christmas Day – here at last!

We thank you for everything that this day means
for the stories and the traditions, and most of all
   for the story of Jesus
who was also called Immanuel – God with us.

God of love, you are here among us, a sleeping child
God with us – here at last
unprotected by cherubim, not throned in splendour,
unaware of shepherd or king
needing a warm bed, a mother's care
needing us as we need you
to live and grow.
It is a great wonder. It is Immanuel – God with us.
We praise you for this wonder!

Sometimes as we prepared for Christmas
we have tried to prepare the way for you

to make a straight road through the world
and smooth out the rough places in our lives
to make your coming easier – but we are still not ready
and you lie in a makeshift cradle
or a cardboard box on a cold pavement
or in the ruins of a bombarded city.

Forgive us that in our excitement we have thought
too much about ourselves, and too little about others.
Forgive our small acts of selfishness
and our immense unconcern for poverty and injustice
that condemn your helpless children to suffering.
Teach us to prepare your way in the world every day
not just at Christmas time.

God loved the world so much that he gave his only son,
that whoever believes in him should not perish, but have
everlasting life. Our sins are forgiven for his sake. Thanks be
to God.

Heather Pencavel

Incarnation

Born
as an innocent Babe,
and wrapped in the swaddling bands
of the world's sorrows and cares.

Born,
not in a palace
but in a hovel.
Not surrounded by servants
and tranquillity –
but by animals,
and noise,
and heaving human activity.

Born,
to bring love,
and hope,
and a new way of living.

Born
as an innocent babe,
and wrapped also in joy
and a belief in humankind
that defies description.

Born
as a single red rosebud
bearing thorns on its stem
with the strength and sharpness
of nails:
bud and thorn holding together
your present innocence
with your future experience.

Susan Hardwick

Joy Abounding

Let all the bells ring with cheerful clangour
and children's laughter echo in the streets
let a cascade of colour greet the day
and harmony of voices join in song
for this is the day to give God glory;
this is the birthday of the King of Kings.

Greeting this day's dawn
the hawk and sparrow sing together,
the fox and hen find common ground;
old enemies can meet each other in friendship;
peace breaks out across the world.
For by this birth the world was freed

of hate and envy, greed and spite,
as God took flesh and pitched a tent on earth.

John Johansen-Berg

Welcome

Jesus, born in poverty,
your shelter inadequate,
shut out, a stranger.

You found no welcome
Bethlehem life went on
as usual, that morning.

All: **Today, once again, we are too busy**
              to notice you,
              alive amongst us.
              Forgive us.

But despite the coldness of our welcome,
You are the one who welcomes us,
each one, to the feast of heaven,
to share the bread of life,
to taste the coming kingdom.

Jesus, you invite us today
to share in the feast that you have prepared for us.

All: **We accept, with thanks.**
              We will come at once.
              Thanks be to you, O God
Amen

Welsh translation on opposite page.

100

Croeso

Iesu, a anwyd mewn tlodi,
mewn llety annigonol, dros dro,
wedi'i gau allan, yn ddieithryn,

'Chest ti fawr o groeso.
Aeth bywyd Bethlehem yn ei flaen
fel arfer, y bore hwnnw.

PAWB: **Heddiw rydym eto yn rhy brysur i sylwi arnat,**
yn byw yn ein mysg.
Maddau i ni.

Ond er ein croeso oeraidd,
Ti yw'r un sydd yn ein croesawu ni,
bob un, i wledd y nefoedd,
i rannu bara'r bywyd,
i flasu'r Deyrnas a ddaw.

Iesu rwyt yn ein gwahodd ni heddiw,
i rannu'r gwledd yr wyt ti wedi'i pharatoi
ar ein cyfer ni.

PAWB: **Fe ddeuwn, heb oedi.**
Derbyniwn gyda diolch,
Diolch mawr I ti, O Dduw.
Amen

Fiona Liddell
Wales

Christ Like!

I open the stable door,
I look into the manger,
I see the child there,
looking just like you.

I give my love as a blanket
to keep you warm
as I discover in you
the Christ of today
and when you cry
I hold you in my arms
and realise
you're just like me.

Richard Becher

Love came down at Christmas –

beginning with the love of two women for their children:
Elizabeth with her cherished child
born in old age;
Mary with her new hopes and dreams
born of a meeting between an angel and a young girl –
hardly more than a child herself.

Love came down at Christmas

in the hearts of an old woman and a young girl.
Together they recognise the wonder
of the God who uses them – the barren one,
the untried girl –
to overturn the powers that be
with their hard eyes and their harsh judgements,
their respect for wealth and their contempt for the poor.

Love came down at Christmas

in the lives of two women:
the clear-eyed love that says Yes
I will do what you ask of me;
the understanding love
that recognises the life of God

102

in the pregnant teenager
and greets her with joy.

Today, God of love, we remember the stories
of all the people who met your love at Bethlehem
and recognised your presence among ordinary folk.

We remember the ones who said Yes to God
Mary who bore him and Joseph who loved her
and her child;
the ones who recognised need and offered shelter;
the ones who understood the importance of the time
and went to look for the baby in the manger;
the ones who travelled in the starlight
looking for a king.

God of yesterday, today and for ever,
help us to see ourselves as we hear their stories.

Show us how to say Yes to you,
whatever it may cost,
Help us to recognise your life
in the weak and the vulnerable ones
we meet day after day.
Teach us to look for you where you are to be found,
among the ordinary folk:
taking shelter with the refugee;
seeking asylum with the displaced ones.

And as we travel our life's road,
show us how to offer our plenty to your need,
our worship to your living presence
and our mortal weakness to your redeeming cross.
Make us part of the Love that came down at Christmas.
In the Name of your Son, who taught us to pray and say

Our Father . . .

Heather Pencavel

Give Thanks to God

Give thanks to God
for the light has come:
    a light in a dark stable,
    a light for darkened lives,
    a light which shines in every place,
    the light of eternal truth.

Give thanks to God
for the truth has come:
    truth that challenges the proud,
    truth that lifts up the lowly,
    truth that brings justice and hope,
    the truth of eternal life.

Give thanks to God
for the life has come:
    the life of God in a new born child,
    life vulnerable and precious,
    life which conquers death's power,
    the new life of the Kingdom of God.

Give thanks to God
for the King has come:
    a King who brings peace,
    a King who brings healing,
    a King who shares our weakness,
    a gentle King whose name is love.

Lord Jesus Christ,
whose coming sets us free,
let your light shine in us,
your truth change us,
your life renew us,

that we may worship you
as the Holy Child of Christmas
and the King of Heaven.

Peter Trow

God With Us

So the Word became flesh; he made his home among us (John 1:14)

Helpless,
vulnerable,
exposed;
a frail human baby born in a cattle shed –
in such a manner
God made his home among us
that we might be drawn to him
through his very defencelessness.

There were none to deny entry
to that Bethlehem stable;
no security locks,
no guards,
no barriers of any kind;
indeed, no Christ,
God came to break all barriers down.

To respond to that love
which risks all in reaching out to us
we surely must also take risks
in reaching out to others.

Risk being misunderstood;
risk having our overtures rejected;
risk becoming vulnerable, defenceless.

How else
can the true Christmas message
be transmitted?
How else
can the word of peace
the word of reconciliation,
become flesh in us?

Edmund Banyard

The Shining Stars Unnumbered

The shining stars unnumbered
  on Bethlehem looked down;
unnumbered, too, the travellers
  who thronged to David's town;
no place to rest, no room to spare,
but what the ox and ass may share
  for Mary's Son so tender;
she laid him in a manger there,
  the Crown of heaven's splendour!

While earth lies hushed and sleeping
  nor dreams of Jesus' birth,
hushed deep in new-born slumbers
  lies he who made the earth;
and from that stable through the night
there shines a lantern burning bright,
  a sign for mortals' seeing,
that Christ is come, the Light of light,
  the Lord of all our being!

A sound of angels singing
  the watching shepherds heard;
our songs of praise are bringing
  anew the promised word;

so let all hearts be joyful when
we hear what angels carolled then
    and tell the Christmas story,
of peace on earth, goodwill to men,
    through Christ the King of glory!

7.6.7.6.8.8.7.8.7 metre

Timothy Dudley-Smith

A World in Pain, a Baby's Cry

A world in pain, a baby's cry;
one dazzling night from times gone by
that gives us Anno Domini:
Year of Our Lord!

A world enslaved, a baby's cry;
the child who spans the earth and sky:
the very man to crucify!
Such love, such woe.

A world of grief, a baby's cry,
so deep our tears, our joy so high:
these things stay with us till we die;
Where is our God?

A world at war, a baby's cry,
the worst, the best, the question why;
what is our hope and our reply?
Jesus is Lord!

A world of sin, a baby's cry;
bad news and good, none can deny,
God with us; God we glorify,
Hallelujah!

Christopher Idle

Child of Bethlehem

Parent-like, they wanted so much for him:
peace and security instead of this rejection,
                    this homeless state:
something better than the pressure of
                    rough wood on gentle flesh.

Child of Bethlehem,
weak and helpless,
have pity on my weakness.

Child of Bethlehem,
loved and cherished,
forgive my lack of love.

Child of Bethlehem,
peaceful in a manger,
calm my restlessness.

Great Son of God made flesh,
hold me in your strong arms.

Raymond Chapman

The New-Born

How one is constantly surprised:
the littleness of the new-born!
Fragile, tough, lying on my arm,
appearing to be deep in thought.
As if, through pain of coming here,
made wise to all earth's grief and joy.
Nothing less than this immense,
this light-creating innocence,
could make the heart's deep darkness sing.

Alan Gaunt

Born Today

The one for whom there was no room is born today.
The Saviour of the world is come to be without a home.
The Word of God is spoken in the weakness of a baby crying,
Made flesh to carry all our endless crosses,
God at our mercy, giving mercy.
Lord how could you do such a thing,
Give such a gift, take such a risk
That we might reject you,
>   spit on you,
>   nail you to a cross,
>   never hear your voice
>   or see your light?

'I am your lover.
I would give myself to you,
and bring my heaven to the darkness of your fearful hell,
and share your flesh and enter all your pain.
I will be with you in the Christ child and the cross.
Though you ignore me, outcast me,
and place me at the margins for a million years,
the light still shines:
until one day you take the baby in your arms,
know me and receive the gift,
love me, and become my child.'

Peter Trow

Christmas Crib

Creator God incarnate
surely an event
to rock the universe,
to stop the heart and still the mind
to silence.
Yet here is no great terrifying stir –
a baby in a stable

a very ordinary-seeming key
to open windows
into eternal mystery.
And you can hardly see the child
for all the creatures round him –
the ox, the ass, the shepherds and the star
and all the known familiar household things.

So here's the truth of incarnation
to find him here
among the gathered folk and all their gear
here where God's strange humility
waits patiently for men to see
waits patiently for all to turn and see
where heaven, where God himself, lies
unobtrusively just within reach.

Order of the Holy Paraclete

Christmas (1)

He came,
Jesus,
so strangely into our world,
so long ago,
so poor,
so helpless.
He came,
and his coming changed our world.
He was an infant,
dependent on his mother
but he was also
our God
and with his coming
a great light has shone
on the people who walked in darkness,
a light that will never be dimmed.

Anthea Dove

Miracle and Magic

God
you could have come
with miracle and magic
in a flash of light
in a hurricane of judgement
so that the earth shook
and the universe trembled
but you chose to come
in a baby's newborn cry
you chose to make your coming known
to working men on a cold hillside
to wandering scholars
to an innkeeper
and to the beasts of the field.

Because you came, a baby,
born to a young girl
you brought miracle and magic and mystery
into ordinary things
and the whole creation sings at your coming
and is blessed.

Heather Pencavel

Scandalous God

Thank you,
scandalous God,
    for giving yourself to the world
    not in the powerful and the extraordinary
    but in weakness and the familiar:
    in a baby; in bread and wine.

Thank you
for offering, at journey's end, a new beginning;
for setting, in the poverty of a stable,
the richest jewel of your love;
for revealing, in a particular place,
your light for all nations . . .

Thank you
for bringing us to Bethlehem, House of Bread,
where the empty are filled,
and the filled are emptied;
where the poor find riches,
and the rich recognise their poverty;
where all who kneel and hold out their hands
are unstintingly fed.

Kate Compston

Vulnerable God

Vulnerable God,
coming in poverty,
forgive us.

Forgive us when we have sought you
in luxury, wealth and power.

We have surrounded you with rich gifts,
we have enthroned you in power,
we have embraced you with comfort.

But you have eluded our grasp.

Help us to find you
in the poor, the weak, the lonely,
in the bareness of the stable,
in the nakedness of birth.

Jan Berry

Northumbrian Nativity

O Lowly Christ
on the darkest night of the year
the Christmas moon
has laid a pathway
across the sea for you
and the lighthouse
beams a welcome.

>As sister moon gives way to brother sun
>the Prince of peace is crowned
>cries of pain give way to tears of joy
>as Mary cradles the whole world in her arms.

A little child, a little child
the living waters of Ezekiel
on Mary's knee,
O Saviour dear,
wise child of Isaiah

>help us to have the humility of the shepherds
>the wisdom of the wise
>the steadfast love of Joseph
>and the courage of Mary.

O Alpha and Omega, on Mary's knee,
as your arm lifts the head of the guilty
help us to forgive.
As your hands caress the face of the poor
help us to seek justice.
As you kiss the leper clean
help us to know your peace.

O little child, root of Jesse,
promised one,
as we leave the stable
as we go from Christmas into the New Year
travel with us.

Kate McIlhagga

A Nativity

Now
    In stillness
        His sun burns off stars,
        Smears a rainbow,
        Wears the veil of dark.

Now
    In quietness
        Each creature imprisons lost dreams,
        Hides from the years,
        Remembers a bidding.

Now
    A hush
        An awesome night beyond night.
        Visible form kisses infinite light:
        Meaning and splendour cry in straw.

Derek Webster

The Christ Child

I'm searching for the Christ child.
It's Christmas time again.
The world is celebrating
will they worship at the crib?

114

I am searching on the city streets
among the lost and homeless.
Surrounded by our Christmas cheer
cold and hungry, blanket wrapped
they struggle for self worth.
The Christ child is not there.

A seller of Big Issue stands outside a superstore.
He is blessed and loved by God
although he may not know it.
The shoppers pass him to and fro
trying not to notice.
Out comes a woman with two bags,
she has felt God's blessing.
She looks right at the seller's face.
'Merry Christmas' she says
handing him a bulging bag and
quickly walks away.
That tough young man holds back a tear
and feels a blessing glow.
The Christ child walked by that day
and many were His blessings.

I am listening to the lonely.
These days of celebration drag
when no one shares them with you.
The TV screen shows laughter, fun.
You turn it off and try to sleep.
It will soon be over.
The Christ child is not there.

Bless those who issue invitations
to join with others in a meal.
Be blessed, accept,
smile and go.
Open up your heart
share His blessings and your love.
You may meet the Christ child there.

The family, we're told
is the place to be at Christmas.
But tensions build and burst
as expectations go astray
and the Christ child seems so very far away.

The shops are full and busy
people rushing, spending, shopping.
We must have this and this and this
and never even stopping
to question 'Why?'
The swish of plastic cards being swiped
drowns out the Christ child's cry.

We sit around our Christmas table
full spread with all delights.
We push away a plate with leavings
that would feed a starving child.
A frown or two, a guilty pang.
The Christ child is not there.

I look into a busy pub
full with young people, laughing.
Drink is flowing, jokes are told
and friends are all together.
The party is loud and noisy.
The Christ child is not there.

Bless those young people
when they leave the pub as they go
to spend time in centres
caring, helping, serving food.
Bless their Christmas time as they give to others.
The Christ child walks by.

A parent in difficulties
dreads this time of year.

Her child will be without
while others have so much.
Life seems unfair and
getting worse.
The Christ child is not there.

Bless those who worship at the cradle
and have found the child.
Bless those who reach for others
and take them by the hand.

Bless those who kneel and worship
and together touch the child.
Bless those who share the hope he brings
and listen to his cry.

Bless all who worship at the cradle
and gaze at the Christ child there.
See hope wrapped up in love so pure
Our God Immanuel.

Jill Denison

Pass-the-Parcel Love:
A Christmas Gift

How could we allow it to happen,
sweet little Jesus-boy?
Allow you to be born
in a bleak down-town-and-out-house?
If only we could say
it was that once-and-only time:
a small lapse in our concentrated gaze
around our needy world.
We certainly could say it –
but we know it not to be true.
It would not convince us;
it certainly would not convince you.

117

Sweet little Saviour-One.
How often we have looked the other way;
walked by on the other side;
shut our minds-doors in the faces
of a modern Mary and Joseph
– swollen-bellied, tear stained and pleading –
declaring that there is no room for them
inside our lives and within our hearts.

Sweet little Holy-Child,
born to give us hope and life
and love beyond description,
lighten our darkness of understanding,
that we may see God's gift
as a pass-the-parcel kind:
not to be hoarded,
but shared –
and unwrapped by <u>all</u>.

Susan Hardwick

Not One Advent

He arrived as a migrant, a wanderer,
looking for a friendly face
in a cold land.

He appeared among us as the preacher
with a new vision
among our battered old altars.

He wore the assorted clothes
and sang the brash songs
that belong to young rebels.

He tottered in with his white stick,
feeling his way over the step,
cautiously finding a seat.

He was setting out the annual plants
in the municipal gardens
when we first saw his face.

We caught a glimpse of him
in a surgeon's mask
when we were caught in that accident.

He arrived as a baby
and we nursed him.

Not one advent, but many, wherever the word
becomes flesh for us.
Come, Lord, here, today,
and open our eyes to see you.

Bernard Thorogood
Australia

When the Child was Born

Where were you
when the child was born?
looking for a way to follow a star,
Seeking a treasure to keep in my heart.

What did you hear
when the child was born?
Singing the love of Mary and Joseph,
Dancing the light with angels above.

What did you see
when the child was born?
Witnessing a piece of Heaven on Earth,
Wondering how God can love me so much.

What did you feel
when the child was born?
Hoping for life for those without hope,
Longing for one who would change our world.

What did you do
when the child was born?
Welcoming the child into my life,
Marvelling at the gift that came to be.

What did you say
when the child was born?
Praying for truth to be known by all,
Thanking the one whose grace makes us free.

What did you give
when the child was born?
Offering my faith to follow his truth,
Awaiting the promise of love without end.

What were you given
when the child was born?
Knowing that I am held in God's love,
Trusting that I am also a gift.

Louise Margaret Granahan
Canada

Carol of the Kingdom

See, now the gates of Heaven stand open wide,
Beside the rough-hewn manger, lay down your pride.
Lay down your worldly wisdom, your spite and scorn –
Here, wrapped in human frailty, your God is born.
Here, in earth's coarse-grained cradle,
Heaven's priceless pearl is laid.
Come, kneel, in wordless wonder,
Be not afraid.

The Kingdom comes among us, unseen, unknown,
No fanfares of procession, no royal throne,
No pomp, nor proclamation, nor sumptuous feast,
The son of heaven's glory lies with the low and least.
Come, in your need and enter
This windswept birthing place.
Receive, without deserving,
God's gift of grace.

Jill Jenkins

Christmas Welcome

The sleighbells sound
a party time
with paper hats,
and baubles
draped on trees of pine,
while churches work
their tireless task
of pointing
out beyond
the glitz and tinsel tinkling
in the lights
towards a starlit cradle scene
beguiling in simplicity:
a baby born to end our night
of doubting.

Pray

Welcome to the prince of peace:
a stable child of royal birth,
within a starlit crisp cold scene
the sound of infant crying heard.
      Welcome child of grace and peace.

Welcome to a mighty Lord:
the humble start belies his strength;
a tender child to change the world,
a challenge to the great and wise.
Welcome child of mighty strength.

Welcome to our lives again:
the ritual festive party sounds
a celebration: voices raise
in songs and psalms and hymns of praise.
Welcome child of love for life.

Stephen Brown

A Prayer to the Christ Child

Lord Jesus, friend to the weary,
be the strength of all who come to you;
Lord Jesus, friend to the sick,
be the healing of all who come to you;
Lord Jesus, friend to the poor,
be the dignity of all who come to you;
Lord Jesus, friend to the excluded,
be the freedom of all who come to you;
until all humans stand renewed before you
and the whole world lives to praise your name.

Christian Aid

Good News for All Humankind

Southern Christmas

The horse flies are buzzing at the wire screen door
and there's a smell of smoke in the air.
The dog lies panting and the flowers droop.
Children splash and shout in the pool
wetting granddad's white trousers
and mother heats the meat pies for lunch,
longing for a rest in the shade of the veranda.

For so long the Christmas imagery has focussed on the north,
with snow on the fir trees, a robin among the holly, a fire in
the grate in the bleak mid-winter. It is a big transition to form
a southern Christmas in our imagination. But perhaps it is
close to reality, for we do not know that Jesus was born in
December and by May the middle East is getting hot. In
December the sheep would have probably been kept indoors
at night, so the narrative may tell us of shepherds in the fields
in spring, at ease under the stars when they heard the singing.

Babe of the sun's warmth, babe of the dust,
the grass is brown and crackles underfoot.
When the cockatoos screech and cicadas chirp
we hear your distant cry of new life
Come in the shade under a great tree,
come in the spray of waves on black rocks,
come as the green pool in the dark gorge,
come as the breeze that ruffles our hair.

You are water in the desert,
oasis of the heart.

You are blossom in the dust,
summer shower.
You are scent of southern summer,
honey in the comb.

Bernard Thorogood
Australia

An Interview with Rajah Khouri

Rajah was born in Jerusalem. When he was one year old, his parents left Jerusalem for Lebanon, expecting to come back soon after, but in the end he did not return to Jerusalem until 1994. He studied at the American University of Beirut and started his business as an architect in the Gulf area. Since 1993 he has been working with the Palestinian Authority in Jerusalem and the Palestinian Territories. He is an optimist.

In an interview in Bethlehem he said:

I look forward to the Christmas season every year. As a Christian, it means a lot to me. Nothing can beat the music of Christmas. I believe the Christmas season is the season for hope, both Advent and Christmas. I have a tradition that I get all my friends together to sing carols. For myself and my children and my family, this is something we'd like to keep on doing – it brings a kind of hope. Then after Christmas, between Christmas and New Year, this is the time when I prefer to remain at home and think about what is happening, what has happened the previous year and what is going to happen next year. I always do that, reviewing the past and thinking of the future.

Garth Hewitt
Christian Aid

At Home in Bethlehem

I have been in the homes of both the rich and poor in Bethlehem. I have been in the mansions of the merchants and olive-wood carvers and I have sat in the homes of people who barely have a door to close against the cold, damp winters of the Judean hills. Yet here in this tiny town, one can still find the Christian faith alive and well, living and breathing in the lives of Arab Christians who make Bethlehem their home. Despite the difficulties of life in this city, I have found people as dedicated to their faith as anyone could hope to find. Regardless of the tragedies, difficulties and obstacles that have beset them, the people of Bethlehem have somehow maintained a glimmer of hope in the midst of hopelessness; joy in the face of despair; and dignity in a part of the world that has denied them recognition for so long.

When I was a child, Bethlehem was a place that existed only in beautifully illustrated pictures of Bible story books – a place that existed far away and was only reflected upon every year as 25 December approached. But here in Bethlehem, the miracle of that first Christmas is remembered every day of the year . . . Bethlehem, spiritual home to Christians the world over, has for the last year been my physical home. Here, in a place that could offer no room for the Christ-child, I have found both room and acceptance from a people who live daily the message brought to earth nearly two thousand years ago.

Douglas Dicks
Bethlehem

Bethlehem

Based on Micah 5:2–5a

Bethlehem:
>place where
>each year, most years,
>ancient hostilities re-surface
>and seem to subvert
>all attempts at paradise-building,
>or endeavours to maintain
>mixed, culturally-enhanced, community life:

Bethlehem:
>place where
>things are as they have always been –
>pregnant with hope
>(after all, an obscure backwater
>has become the focus of world attention!)
>However abused the fact down the ages,
>the boy, Jesus, was born.

>**In religious wrangles and political upheavals,**
>**claim and counter-claim,**
>**whenever human feelings run high,**
>**remind us, Jesus,**
>**your peace embodies justice.**

Bethlehem,
>place of Jesus' birth,
>of busy markets
>and bright lights in heaving streets:
>place of historical insignificance,
>and world-wide Christian adoration;
>cited by the prophet, Micah;
>almost unnoticed,
>and now, at Christmas,

crammed with television cameras
beaming midnight carols by satellite
instantly
across the world.

**In religious wrangles and political upheavals,
claim and counter-claim,
whenever human feelings run high,
remind us, Jesus,
you are the one of peace.**

Pamela Turner

Christmas in Nazareth

The changes of the seasons were always exciting, like a ritual
in our lives as a family and as a community. When winter
came, it gave us such joy to come back from school to a cosy
home. In the evening, my mother would boil carrots and roast
chestnuts on the brazier while we sat on floor mattresses
and cushions or on low wicker chairs. We would also have
plates of dried figs, raisins and walnuts. As a child I did
not like autumn, a melancholy season, but then I began to
look forward to Christmas. In Nazareth, Christmas was more
low-key than Easter, which was and still is called the Great
Feast. There were Christmas trees in public buildings and in
some (mainly Protestant) churches and church schools.
Catholic churches put more emphasis on the crib and the
stable-cave.

I should mention that the Western communities in
Nazareth followed the well-known Julian calendar, while the
Eastern churches followed their own calendar, so that
Western Christmas was on 25 December, while the Orthodox
Christmas was on 6 January. Sometimes there might be a
whole forty days between the Orthodox and Western Easters.

Epiphany fell on 6 January, the Greek Orthodox Christmas.
Special sweets were prepared with very thin pastry, some of

127

it filled with nuts, cinnamon and sugar and some fried and dipped in syrup. On 15 January, it was my brother Irfan's birthday. All our extended family would come for a big tea and my father engaged the best sweet-maker to come to the house and prepare two huge trays of *kenafeh* (shredded rolls of wheat with syrup, cheese or walnuts). My mother played the organ and we all sang hymns, followed by games. After my brother's birthday, my mother would take down the Christmas tree and the Christmas decorations were put away for another year, *inshallah* (God willing).

Najwa Farah
Nazareth

Seeing the Christmas Christ

Dear friends,

I can offer you no more real, human, honest, searing and wondrous Christmas thoughts than this message from a priest I am privileged to know, who works in an AIDS clinic in a developing country. Last Holy Thursday he and his friend visited a prison on the other side of the country. This Christmas he visited it again. I do not know what it means to believe that Divine Love is made incarnate in a world filled with places like this. I don't know what it means to sing of hope and peace in the almost unbearably harsh reality lived by those who are counted as worthless. Perhaps the people in this prison could teach me a little about it. But I do know this – the carols we sing before the manger are empty unless our hearts are broken open by the knowledge that children are still lying in mangers like these. May that knowledge, may the songs that parents sing to their children in these Bethlehems transform our hearts and open us to the shock and the scandal of God made flesh. In joy and hope.

A Friend

December in an African Prison

As always, the trip to the prison today remains beyond description. I can't even attempt to write this without tears in my eyes. After coming away, my friend and I are simply emotionally drained. We've seen hell. And I mean hell. How often have I used the term 'hell on earth', but believe me, the inside of prison puts new meaning into that concept and it is beyond any possible conception you might even think you have. The overcrowding was so incredible, that all we could bring to the men is a bar of soap . . . over 3,000. The warden and staff were quite suspicious, but breaking all rules, allowed us into the prison to distribute the soap. We also stocked the prison dispensary with hundreds of dollars' worth of medicines. After the men's side, we went to the women's side of the prison. There are far less women in prison, so they each got soap and a piece of fruit. Now, the heart stopper . . . within the women's prison were ten children born while these women were incarcerated, children who have never been outside the prison walls. Children who have never had a toy. We had some small stuffed animals and each kid got a stuffed animal. A few cried, as they were afraid at first as they had never seen anything like this stuffed thing we were trying to give them. Others just smiled with stars in their eyes at receiving perhaps their first gift ever and then the women gathered in song to thank us.

And then it hit me. This mystery of the three wise men, magi, astronomers from the East. Our carols and stories and traditions have grown in 2,000 years, so that I really wonder what their gifts meant to these two poor unmarried teenagers who just gave birth to their son in an animal shelter. I wonder what gifts they really brought. Perhaps a few simple stuffed toys. Because what we both remarked to each other on the long, bumpy drive back from the prison, is that we really didn't go there for the prisoners. And we know that. Yes, there's a value in giving each inmate a bar of soap. Yes, there's a value that these most forgotten people know that at least a few people remembered them today. But we got far more out

129

of our visit today, than we could ever give. Because in the midst of that prison, in the filth, the stench, the most severe poverty and inhumane conditions I've ever witnessed, I understand the world our Saviour chose to be born into. To each of those children who received a stuffed toy, we were the 'strange visitors from the west'. But we saw the Christ Child . . . living, breathing, walking, smiling, crying and alive in the hell hole of that prison. No gift that anyone gives me, no meal I share during the next couple of days can compare to what the men and women of the prison gave to me today . . . I have glimpsed again at God . . . I have seen Jesus . . . and he lives . . . in that prison.

Love,

For security reasons all names of people and actual locations have been removed.

An African Country

A Visit to Reading Prison on Christmas Day

Many bishops visit a prison on Christmas Day to celebrate the Eucharist.

Thanks are given that God has come among us in the life of Jesus Christ.

Joy . . . because of the occasion.

Sadness . . . because prisoners are separated from their families on Christmas Day.

Each year I go to Reading Prison (still known locally as Reading Gaol of Oscar Wilde fame). It is now a young offenders' prison and remand centre.

As the young offenders kneel at the altar rail, the prison governor always kneels among them to receive communion with them.

For me, that simple action speaks of what Christmas is all about.

Dominic Walker

Someone Who Has Become a Friend

I entered the dirty lift within the estate building
Ten storeys high – home for alcoholics, down-and-outs, the
    lonely.
And other strugglers, in Belfast's loyalist territory
Near where murder and mayhem had recently raged
And I took gifts for someone who has become a friend
a man poor in worldly advantages,
physically deformed, vision limited
who has a sharp mind,
a desire for friendship and dignity.

In his rough room with bare minimum furniture,
Next to nought in cupboards,
He sat, weeping as he unwrapped
Gifts, practical and funny.
'Give me a hug,' he said. I embraced his bent form
and felt God's love for him.
A little radio, his regular friend,
Was propped close to his chair and there I left him
Returning to comfort and cheer,
The better for knowing him . . . and a little ashamed.
He is invited to our Christmas dinner.
He will not come – too much provision overwhelms.

Glenn Jetta Barclay
Aotearoa New Zealand/Northern Ireland

Christmas by the Roadside

The children could hardly wait . . . they could smell the cake
cooking and knew there was going to be a party. The worship
was lively and everyone took part in the service. We had a
live nativity scene, because we don't have any figures – we
just used the children in the camp. Children dressed up as
Mary and Joseph, the wise men and the shepherds. We had
a Christmas tree in the camp which we covered with

decorations – they were very poor. We used all we had. We made paper chains and hung pine cones, ribbons and any Christmas cards we received on the tree. It was very beautiful.

Denise Gomes de Amorim
Christian Aid, Brazil

Joselie's Dream

Joselie and her family live in a tiny wooden shack roofed with black plastic sheeting. When it rains mud is washed through the house, underneath the bed and table and out the other side. They live in a camp next to a huge area of unused land.

The Brazilian government says the people in the camp have the right to farm this land but the families have been waiting for two years for the paperwork to be finished so that the land can be officially allocated to them. Only then will they be able to build a proper house, send the children to school and unpack the toys. Joselie's family is one of the 4.8 million families in Brazil who have no land on which to grow food. Forty-four per cent of the land in Brazil is owned by just one per cent of its people. The Movement of the Landless has helped over 120,000 families to establish ownership of land through long and time-consuming paperwork.

Joselie chased around the field trying to follow the butterflies that were darting over the corn. She could see the bent figures of her parents in the distance collecting food for the family's cows and pigs. Her mother straightened up and looked in Joselie's direction.

'Keep an eye on your sister!' she called.

Joselie was a year older than her five-year-old sister Josemere, who was resting under the shade of a nearby tree looking after a cow. She held onto the cow's reins and sang a song to pass away the time. Soon Joselie would go and play with her. Meanwhile Joselie would make the most of the peace and quiet and be on her own. She ran to the little play house of corn sheaves she had made for herself. She was very proud of it and no-one else was allowed to go inside. It had a door and two windows. Inside were a bed, table, chairs and an oven which were all made from green stems.

Today Joselie just felt like dreaming. She sat alone, except for Teddy, her ragged and battered friend. Much of his stuffing had long ago been washed away in the mud. Although she loved Teddy, she thought about the brand new toys given to her last Christmas. They were still in their wrappings in the roadside shack which was the family home. They hung from the rafters to stop them from being washed away in the rain and storms that so often ruined everything.

'One day we shall have a real home,' sighed Joselie as she dreamed of the brick house that her father was going to build. She tried to picture the home for which they had waited so long. She and Josemere had been promised a proper bedroom. She imagined waking up on Christmas morning in their very own bunk bed. There would be decorations everywhere which she would help to make.

A Prayer

With open hands we offer to God our prayers and our gifts.
We remember especially those by the roadsides of Brazil
waiting to go home for Christmas.
Let these prayers and the gifts of many help to strengthen
   their leadership,
give health for their children,
deliver them from violence and from danger on the roads,
enlighten governments so that they look to people in
   despair,
give courage to those who want to give up
and help those who are suffering to smile.

Christian Aid
Brazil

A Korean Welcome

Many of the customs which have developed around Christmas in Korea focus on welcoming new people and making friends with strangers.

Christmas Eve

Celebrations begin on Christmas Eve when friends are invited to a special evening service. A child of about three years of age starts the service by welcoming everyone. The service is a joyful time and includes drama, carols, dance, readings and prayers. Afterwards everyone, including the visitors, stays for a party.

Here is Yo Hwan's account of what happens next:

'After getting home late last night we got up at 04.00 this morning! Then we go carol singing. My Dad was carrying a sack. As we went around to people's homes they came out, listened to us and then put small parcels of sweets into the sack. When we got back we had a sack full of sweets. Later we went to church. The children had their own service and afterwards all the sweets were given out to them. Then we stayed to eat rice cakes together before going home to bed.'

Yo Hwan's parents grew up in the country where churches are few and far between. As they walked the two-hour journey they would sing:

Christmas Greetings

Christmas bells do ring, ring, ring,
Hear the gentle far off sound,
Call clearly o'er the mountains
To the distant cottage,
Christmas greetings to us all.

Christmas bells do ring, ring, ring,
Hear the gentle far off sound,
Call clearly o'er the wide sea
To the people fishing,
Christmas greetings to us all.

Christmas bells do ring, ring, ring,
Hear the gentle far off sound,
They say to all God's children
Send the world your greetings,
Jesus Christ is born today.

Christian Aid
Korea

The Incarnation of Christ for the Entire World:
Aspects from Palestine

Christmas comes to tell us the story of God's indwelling among us. Few people would deny that we cannot tell stories of God in himself but as he is revealed to us in history and in human stories. The revelation of God is always in history and not beyond history. Faith 'came' into history (Galatians 3:23). Human experience is necessarily the proper arena for divine revelation as it is for any kind of revelation. The measure of our humanity tells us that we can receive what is disclosed only through the medium of our experience.

In the history of Jesus of Nazareth, the Church, slowly but powerfully, discovered the faith of the Incarnation. The man Jesus with all his deeds, words and his consequent destiny, was an utterance of God. God's Word did something and does something today and always.

The revelation of God is thus proclaimed through the human word which becomes the graced opportunities of a new beginning for others. And so, when we confess loudly our faith in him who for us and for our salvation came down from heaven and was incarnate by the Holy Spirit of the Virgin Mary and was made man we confess a central moment

135

in our creed however difficult and tantalizing to understand.

Christmas tells us the story of God's faithfulness to us. God's love for us is the means by which the seemingly impossible is done as the Evangelists witness in the birth narratives. Love is the one thing that makes all things possible. It transforms people's lives and brings life in place of death; it heals the deepest wounds. Love performs miracles. And Jesus' birth is a miracle; he is a totally unpredictable surprise caused by the power of love, so that not even the physical initiative of a human father can be thought of as complementing the divine act that brings Jesus into being.

However, to look at a story of someone we need to look at the story in its entirety. The miracle of Christmas is indeed the story of God's faithfulness. However, it is the story of God's vulnerable faithfulness. So soon after the scene of angelic hosts and shepherds, the prayerful gathering about a manger, we are confronted with the harsh reality that this birth, this child, was not desired. When the plans of the powerful to find the particular failed, they resorted to mass execution. Hence, Holy Innocents Day. We in Palestine like to remind people that: 'Nothing is new under the sun.' Our children are still killed today, albeit by a different Herod, and the Palestinian Rachel continues to weep even today. The name of the babe Jesus becomes the name of all the lost, all the forgotten and all the martyred.

God's faithfulness and glory at Christmas are not simply the result of God's power. They are bought at a price – the price of the violence unleashed in the cross of Jesus. The cross is the ultimate expression of the power of mercy and of love, as opposed to the desires and arrogance of religious and political powers and systems.

We continue to believe that the biblical drama is still going on. Truly, Faith is that which applies to all in every land of every language; but the vividness of the biblical story continues to show forth God's story and life in the lives of our communities and our people here in the land of the Holy One. The suffering that has been caused upon the Palestinians and the Palestinian Christians particularly is so intense. The killing of our own children and the evacuation of people from their homes and properties by the power of military shelling and mortars is again a sharp reminder of the story of Jesus. Mary and Joseph may have had to avoid checkpoints of Roman soldiers. We wonder whether they would have been let into Bethlehem as they would have had to go through Israeli checkpoints today.

The actors change but the plot remains the same. It is not unwise, therefore, that the Church decided to celebrate St Stephen's Day, the day after the celebration of the Nativity of our Lord. It reminds us all, wherever we may be, of the cost of discipleship. Following Christ as Lord is not now, and never has been, without consequence. Celebrating Christmas in Bethlehem and in his land means also sharing in his sufferings and death.

However, in some countries, Christians have the luxury of finding their faith easy to bear, some even find it easy to ignore. But in other countries and they are many, not least here in Palestine, Christians face intense challenges for who they are. The Christian presence which has been here in this land since the first Pentecost has been put under the gravest jeopardy. The Church built of living stones, of apostles, teachers and evangelists to tell the message of Christmas has been slowly perishing, for many reasons, not least political discrimination and the inability to live with dignity and liberty as children of God. But, also, we believe that in him even death becomes invested with God's mercy. For he has deigned to share our humanity so that we may share in his divinity. God and man are brought together in that space of history in those short years in Palestine so that history is the sign that interprets all history. And by his death all death is conquered.

Christmas is the season when God shows that he is a giving God by whom the whole world is sustained by mercy and generosity without limit. As the Body of Christ, we too are called to live as members of one another, to listen to each other's needs and concerns and come to show solidarity

137

expressed in understanding one another's humanity. The Christians of Bethlehem and of the land of the Holy One have been very grateful for the solidarity of many around the world; but also plead that their story is heard and shared by all who call themselves Christian.

Our prayers and hopes are that God will continue to renew his creation through Christ and by the power of the Holy Spirit, that by the power of his love, he will heal the wounds of division between all who live in this land so that his glory may shine and the angelic hymns abound for ever and eternity.

The Rt Revd Riah Abu El-Assal
Anglican Bishop in Jerusalem

Stars and Angels,
Shepherds and Kings

Let Us Go and See

Luke 2:15

'Let us go and see,' was the immediate response the shepherds made after being told by the angels that the Saviour of the world had been born in Bethlehem. One wonders who was then responsible for the sheep that were being looked after by them.

What about the time they started off?

Were they not risking their lives by travelling during the night?

What about the distance they had to cover to get to the birthplace of Jesus?

Did they use any means of transport or had they to go on foot?

What about their ages – were they young and athletic?

It is difficult to answer these questions. But one thing is certain, the joyful message from the angels had quickened them to go to Bethlehem. They could not wait to see and pay homage to the Saviour of the world. I am sure seeing him in the stable was not an end in itself but gladly they went back to their various homes sharing Good News with everybody they met on the way.

How many times have we been challenged by the power of the Good News to go out and see what is happening in our communities?

Do we hear the voices calling for help?

Voices crying for shelter, food, peace and justice?

Or do we first think of our security and cost whatever that may be?

Maybe we don't hear any voices because the 'walls' of our churches are so thick?

Remember the shepherds did not hesitate but with enthusiasm they went out and witnessed to the birth of Our Lord. Do we have the same enthusiasm to go out and witness the same Good News to others in our communities today?

'Let us go and see, let us go and share.' So I say.

Goodwin Zainga
Malawi

Stars and Angels

Is that a star
that steady-moving light
or pseudo-star projecting stars
of stage and screen
to entertain and titillate
consumption-weary minds?
Is that a star?

Is that an angel
that soft seductive voice
promising bliss – sun and blue sky,
a top-range car,
fortune (it could be me!)
paradise – and at such little cost?
Is that an angel?

The star shines clear
above a shelter on a city street
where lies a child caught in a web
of poverty, helpless and innocent
victim of powerful people's greed.
There shines the star.

The angel speaks
to workers in the fields
(or in the kitchens of the noisy inn)
bringing news of peace on earth
with justice and goodwill to humankind.
There speaks the angel.

God of the real, the true,
speak through your living Word
and show us how
to see the artificial for itself
and in today's real world
to recognise the angel and the star.

And suddenly there was with the angel
a multitude of the heavenly host
praising God and saying
Peace on earth and good will to all people!
For unto you is born this day in the City of David
a Saviour . . . and you will find the babe lying in a manger.

Heather Pencavel

Inside Out?

Christmas is outside in!
The characters in the familiar
nativity scene all come
in from the outside.

Shepherds come,
from outside the city,
despised by the righteous people
because their work keeps them outside
the religious in-crowd;
outsiders spending their nights vulnerable
with their flocks,
no one to watch over them.

Wise men come,
wealthy and learned,
but outsiders too.
Strangers in a strange land,
foreigners in odd clothes,
treated with suspicion;
'not really like us'.

Mary and Joseph come,
Galileans, outsiders,
'nothing good comes from there you know!' –
travellers with no package tour,
no hotel reservations.
Are they refused room
because they speak with strange accents?
because they are poor?
because she is pregnant?

Jesus comes,
born an outsider,
living with outsiders,
touching outsiders,
lepers and gentiles,
sinners and prostitutes:
dying as he is born,
outside the city,
on the rubbish dump.

Christmas is for the outsiders:
the ones who need God with them
because they have no one else;
because people fear them
shun them, and shut them outside.

Are we outsiders?

If we recognise our need,
put aside our self sufficient pride,
and admit
that when the darkest night
surrounds us
and we feel the cold draughts
of hatred or indifference
we are afraid, and cannot find
the candle flame within us
to light our path to safety,

then we have
prepared a place of welcome
for the Light that comes,
the Word that speaks our hope and peace,
the One who opens the door,
bringing outsiders in
to warm themselves
at the fire of God's passionate love –

and Christmas is for us.

Peter Trow

Can You Hear the Angels Singing?

Listen!
Can't you hear the angels singing
where the ordinary people go about their business?
As much in the office or factory
the busy shopping precinct
the suburban home
the sheltered flat
as on a Bethlehem hill
the angels' song is ringing.

The message is not exclusively for shepherds,
though to hear it needs an ear attuned
to the unexpected undertones of hope.
All are invited to join the headlong rush,
to see what the God of Love has done:
a baby laid in a manger.

This is an eternal song,
but here and now it is sung for us.
For a moment heaven has come to earth,
and we share the wonder and the worship
of the angel choirs.

The Child will grow to bear a cross
and then, at last, the fragile curtain
which hides the holy place will be torn away.
The glory of heaven and the peace of earth
are inseparably joined in him.
For him the music of creation harmonises with
the praise of all that lives.

Listen, can you hear angels singing?
Will you raise your voice and join the song?

Peter Trow

Bethlehem, Bethlehem

Bethlehem, Bethlehem
Young Mary went down to Bethlehem
Bethlehem, Bethlehem
City of our Saviour's birth

Shepherds come, shepherds come
The shepherds come down to Bethlehem
Shepherds come, shepherds come
Witness to our Saviour's birth

Angels say, angels say;
Be not afraid down in Bethlehem
Angels say, angels say
Herald to our Saviour's birth

Jesus come, Jesus come
Christ born today down in Bethlehem
Jesus come, Jesus come
Child of the Lord most high.

Michael Jacob Kooiman
Canada

How Far is It to Bethlehem?

As to the distance: it depends
on where you are when you set out.
Naturally. If the winds
of heaven take up the slack, make taut
your soul, make winged your feet,
so that you soar –
singing your heart's true song,
following the crumb-trail of your star –
the journey will not be long;
for the House of Bread is where you are
but have not tasted, savoured, taken in, before.

I say; the journey will not be long,
but you will have ventured all and travelled far . . .

Kate Compston

We, Too, are Shepherds

The angel danced and laughed
and touched my eyes
And the world lit like Christmas,
A depth of sparkling lights,

everywhere, the touch of God,
Lightness of Spirit
Shining back to me.

I felt like a child
discovering Christmas is true,
Barely daring to believe,
Hesitant to even move
in case the glory should vanish,
But the angel laughed and danced on
And the world stood new-made.

Wendy White

Christmas (2)

Christmas here in England's when the stars
pierce frost-hard, cloud-clear night
with diamond light;
when
Holly's massed and sombre, spiky leaf
defends, with dark green art,
a crimson heart;
when
Robins bounce like feather balls, spark-bright,
on twig-thin legs, eyes bold,
alive with cold;
when
Ice and sunlight flash, and morning trees
are tinselled ghosts that peer
through milk-white air;
when
Snow, in layers of silence, settles deep,
to wait the cries that break
as children wake.
Ah,

146

Time and distance hide that other world,
that dusty, foreign scene
in Palestine,
where
Mary found, with Joseph, stable-room,
to rest her – travel worn –
till Babe was born.
Then
Angel song and strange light filled the sky,
as Great God sleeping lay
on manger hay,
and
Shepherds came, and Princes left their thrones,
honour and gifts to bring
Lord Christ the King.

Paul Hampton

The Gift

Mary came riding,
riding on a donkey
riding to Bethlehem,
carrying God's gift to the world.

Joseph came walking,
walking by Mary
walking to Bethlehem,
caring for God's gift to the world.

Shepherds came running,
running in obedience
running to Bethlehem,
worshipping God's gift to the world.

Wise men came travelling
seeking, following
the bright star to Bethlehem,
finding God's gift to the world.

Will you come riding
walking or running?
will you come seeking
following, finding?

Heather Johnston

Star Light

Deep through the forest, the wise man comes riding;
High on the saddle, he looks to the sky;
follows the star where its bright light is pointing;
fears no robber, nor wild wolvish cry.
Far he has journeyed, through city and village,
braving the winds and deep winter's cold;
an old man with visions who looks for a baby,
to bring to its cradle an offering of gold.

Crossing the desert, a wise man comes riding,
shading his eyes from the wind and the dust.
Why should he travel on such a great journey?
He cannot explain it; he does what he must.
Far from home country, he rides by the star-light,
follows its guiding to Bethlehem town.
When he has entered, in lowly devotion,
his incense for Jesus he'll gladly lay down.

High on the mountains, a wise man comes riding;
black is his face and black is the night.
Steeply descending, yet fearing no danger,
so sure is the guidance of star's radiant light.

This is a man who has left eastern splendour,
to follow a vision in catching a star.
Down from the mountain the star brings him safely,
to give to his Saviour an offering of myrrh.

Straight to the stable the wise men come riding,
sharp on the night, the hooves ringing clear.
Right to the manger, the star's light is guiding;
then enter quite softly; the Christ child is here.
Down on their knees, the three gaze in wonder,
the star and the Saviour, as they were told.
Opening their treasures, they give to the baby,
frankincense, perfume and casket of gold.

John Johansen-Berg

The Christmas Rap

The style of this presentation is inspired by the rhythms of the Caribbean and reflects the idea of using distinctive rhythms.

Group A It's the Christmas rap
Group B Da doo dn doo dn
Group A It's the Christmas Rap
Group B Da doo dn doo dn
Group A It's the angel rap
Group B Da doo dn doo dn
Group A It's the angel rap
Group B Da doo dn doo dn
Group A It's the rap.

Angels *(Two groups of four enter and sing the Christmas Rap. Short silence then recommence clicking. When the speaking starts let the words carry the rhythm or use a drum or another percussion instrument to maintain the rhythm)*

Come on everybody, we've a story to tell
'Bout a baby called Jesus, his parents as well,
Some kings and some shepherds, and innkeepers
   too
And the animals with them . . .

Chaz   *(Entering)* But not in a zoo. *(Stands at the end of a group of angels)*

Angels   That's Chaz, please ignore him, he's just full of fun
Let's get this rap started, let's get this job done!

(Sing the Christmas Rap. Finger clicking stops at the end)

Mary   *(Entering with Joseph)*

Oh! Joseph, I'm tired! We've come a long way.
I can feel the babe jumping; let's call it a day.
I'll sit here to rest now, down here on the ground,
While you find us lodgings; while you look
   around.

(Joseph pats her shoulder and walks off the stage. Mary sits stage left and rests)

Chaz   *(Walks forward and talks to audience)*

Look at her resting, she seems so frail.
But her spirit is stronger than a hurricane gale.
Poor Joseph is older; he's tired too.
And I'd love to help, but what can I do?

(Shrugs, starts to walk away. A child runs on and bumps into Chaz)

Chaz   Hey!

150

Child *(Runs off but shouts back)*

Sorry!

Crowd Scene *(People enter and some of them are carrying goods to sell. They call to each other, asking about lodgings, complaining about the long journeys and the bureaucrats who have called the census. Make the scene fun and allow the actors to work out their own dialogue. Chaz is hustling about in the crowd)*

Chaz The people are crowding, I'm all black and blue.
I know what I'll do now, I'll sit here with you.

(Sits down with the audience, and looks on)

Crowd *(People talk about the rush of tourists, the lack of rooms, the census. The scene is not in rap rhythm)*

Angels *(Sing the Christmas Rap through twice. During the second singing they move towards the audience and invite people to join in)*

Joseph *(Enters, looks at Mary and speaks to the audience)*

Poor Mary is tired but we must move on.
All the rooms have been hired, no room for my
    son.

(Feigns cheerfulness and turns to Mary)

Come with me Mary and see what I've found.
There are inns and some people, let's look around.
We'll go to this inn now and give it a try.

(Mary rises and Joseph turns to the audience)

Perhaps there'll be room here for Mary to lie.

151

Chaz	(*Stands up and peers around at the audience with a hand over his eyes*)
	You must be joking! (*Sits down*)
Joseph	(*Knocks on imaginary door which is close to and facing the audience. No response*)
Angel One	(*Steps out of the chorus, walks forward, taking off the halo or a part of the costume to become an ordinary person*)
	Now Chaz, do get going! Take a part in our play. We're short of an actor. Be the landlord! OK?
	(*Angel stands to one side*)
Chaz	(*Stands up, look around and speaks in a different voice*)
	Hello there, and welcome. But I'm sorry to say That my inn is all hired. I've no room today!
	(*Gestures toward audience*)
	You can see how we're packed from the ceiling to the floor People standing in aisles and blocking the door.
Joseph	We came for the census, to Bethlehem city And hoped to find shelter, but can't. It's a pity! This place is so busy! Where can Mary rest? I don't even know what to do for the best.
Angel One	(*Stands, nods, looks sympathetic*)
Chaz	Wait a minute! Poor Mary, I can't let that pass.

I've a stable to shelter my ox and my ass.
It's old and it's crumbling, there isn't a door.
But it's dry and it's clean and there's a bedding
  of straw!
I'd be sorry, you see, not to welcome a stranger
And Mary can put the new babe in the manger.
Come this way. Follow me and you'll find peace
  and calm.
With my animals you will be safe from all harm.

Angels *(Cheer and clap as Chaz leads Mary and Joseph out)*

Angel One *(Walks forward and calls after them)*

Well done Chaz! That was great! You helped
  finish our story
And your acting was great!

Chaz *(Sticks head around the door)*

Now I'm covered in glory.

Angels *(Start to finger click the Christmas Rap)*

Angel One Glory? Oh no! Wait for me!

(Runs to join the angels)

Angels *(Sing the Christmas Rap)*

Angel One While Mary and Joseph had gone to the stable
The angels had sung to those who were able
To gather the sheep. Tell them Jesus was born.
They'd be first to visit him that Christmas morn.
Ordinary people like you and me

153

Were the very first people that Jesus did see.
The wise and the rich men, they followed after
To share in the story and join in the laughter.

Angels   *(Quietly and prayerfully sing the Christmas Rap. If available, a Nativity Tableau can be focussed on, otherwise Mary and Joseph walk to their positions)*

All   *(After a short pause sing 'Away in a Manger' or another suitable carol. During the singing everyone is invited on to the stage to stand, sit or kneel. Everyone becomes a part of the tableau)*

Chaz   *(Clearly and with confidence)*

I've joined in the acting, been watching the play.
And now in the stable lies the child in the hay.
I want to visit him, join in the fun,
Because this miracle has only begun.
This young child calls us all to his side
And welcomes us all this Christmastide.
Feed the poor, heal the sick. Come be part of the
tale.
This way of loving, never can fail!

Angels   *(Sing the Christmas Rap. Repeat after the last line and add 'That's a rap!' Finish with a loud 'Yeah' shooting hands up into the air. Encourage the audience to join in with shakers, streamers and singing)*

Margery Robinson
Christian Aid
Scotland

A Gospel Reflection

Luke 2:8–20

When we find the baby, when we nourish our inner child, we will hear the Song of the Universe. We only hear that song when our hearts are open to wonder, the wonder we see in the eyes of a child, the wonder we experience when we see God in a helpless baby.

O Divine Musician of the spheres, still our restlessness and silence our chatter that like the shepherds of old we may transform every oppression into a Bethlehem.

W. L. Wallace
Aotearoa New Zealand

Pondering These Things

Nativity Gift List

Dear God
please give me

the unquestioning faith of Mary
the tolerance of Joseph
the patience of the donkey
the kindness of the innkeeper
the reverence of the oxen
the joy of the angels
the obedience of the shepherds
the perseverance of the wise men

the Christ-child in my heart today

Heather Johnston

Unwrap the Gift

The love of Christ is a gift
But it doesn't come
All wrapped up with paper and string
And we don't say:
Just what I always wanted
To put in the hall, or to wear or to eat,
Or do nothing at all with
But just look and enjoy.

We can't put it aside until next year,
Just bringing it out for special events:
To celebrate, Christmas or Easter or Lent.

There isn't a place in the house
To put it away or to leave it alone:
The life of Christ wants our lives as a home.

The life of Christ is a call
Whispering in the night
Crying out through the day
Sometimes coming quite suddenly to say:
'Look at this some other way'.
Don't think it's enough, just to sing and to pray
Don't think it's enough just to mean what you say
Hoping for the best as you turn away.

We can't turn it off
When it's too hard to think
Hoping to be let off the hook.
We have to face things
That leave us confused
To see them head on we must look.

The life of Christ is a dare.
Do we dare? How dare we dare?
Could we dare without anything there?
The word of the past and the future is now
It's a fight and a strain as we try to know how
To live smack up against the challenge of now.

There's no little room where the light doesn't reach
No space of my own, where only my thoughts
Have a power and a place.
No look in the mirror to see my own face
And to wonder just 'how do I seem?'
The eyes and the ears and the lives
That are opened look out –
They don't need to look in!

Virginia Becher

Christmas Card

The medieval Christmas view,
with angels poised above the crib,
and beasts immaculate who stand
around the pristine sleeping babe:
       sing Gloria.

The cherubs blow, their trumpets gleam,
and on the distant town the sun
shines gold on turrets, gates and walls
while zephyrs ruffle white dove wings:
       sing Gloria.

The pavement's hard, the gutter filled
with refuse, gates are shut and barred.
They queue at one tap's miser drip
for solace in Calcutta heat,
and care for new life lying there,
this babe who fights for breath and hope.
       Sing Gloria, sing Peace.

Bernard Thorogood
Australia

Christmas is a Time for . . .

Christmas is a time for celebration,
to spread love, to offer friendship, for reconciliation.

Christmas is a time for reflection,
to illuminate hope, to alleviate suffering, for communication.

Christmas is a time for edification,
to raise spirits, to wear a smile, for association.

Christmas is a time for revelation,
to discard hidden motives, to display honesty, for unification.

Christmas is a time for happiness,
to wash away sorrow, to embrace a neighbour, for tenderness.

Christmas is a time for giving,
to accept gifts, to give thanks, for living.

Christmas is a time to cast differences aside,
to pardon transgression, to forget grievances, to abandon
foolish pride.

Christmas is a time to remember,
all the children of God who are suffering in December.

Christmas is a time to praise the Lord, for the beauty of
creation and His infinite love and compassion.

Christmas is a time to think of Christ upon the Cross
and the sacrifice He made so that we could celebrate
Christmas.

Jason Doré

On Christmas Day

Shall we look back to summer when
warmth lay deeply drifted or forward into
spring, savouring a foreseeable future of
exquisite natural beauty?

Shall we search vainly for words or for
pictures to distil for us the small, bright
centre of truth we love,
so that we may hold on to and draw strength from it?

How shall we try to touch once more
the hidden heart, lest we drown at last in
a sea of shame and disenchantment?

159

Is the gold there, after all, in the
little Jewish Child,
and in the world's fading memory of him –
a simple present that we've overlooked?

Paul Hampton

Christmas Day

On such a day as this
there is within me
a place – some holy say
where I belong.

A day
where quantum mysteries
and Gaian deities,
New Age crystallogies
and Trinitarian niceties
with filofactic fripperies
just melt away.

A place – a day
where I
with children
like to play.

Erna Colebrook

Christmas Time

I can remember my childhood Christmas.
The presents underneath the decorated tree.
Expectantly I waited, hoping eagerly
For the presents that were meant for me.

I can remember those Christmas times.
Opening the presents that were labelled mine.

Trying to hide the painful disappointment
For the presents never satisfied the hopes.

I can remember one Christmas time.
The year that Father Christmas disappeared.
My parents must have bought the gifts
For the presents were devoid of love.

I can remember a different Christmas time.
Receiving presents that were meant for me.
It was the best time of my life,
For the presents came with love from God.

I will remember every Christmas time,
There is a decorated wooden cross,
God gave the world his only Son
His present, full of love, to me.

Frances Ballantyne

What's on Tonight?

There's never much to watch on Christmas night
we're too full up to care in any case – no tea, thank you
a mince pie is all that I can take just now
sugary and soft with that rich brandy taste.
Switch on the telly – see what's on tonight.

The News – not much to tell on Christmas Day
the Queen, of course, wishing us better times
and Bethlehem, pilgrims in Manger Square
and somewhere Jews and Palestinians fight –
there's never much to watch on Christmas night.

What next? – a sitcom Christmas special, I suppose.
I don't believe it! Try the other side –
blue sea and golden beaches – it's an ad

161

for holidays next year: let's finish this one first –
there's never much to watch on Christmas night.

That's better now – someone to make us laugh
nothing too risque, just a bit near the edge;
BBC 2's got poems by Betjeman
it's either that or Christmas with the stars –
there's never much to watch on Christmas night.

God whose light shines unheeded in the world
forgive the blindness of our shallow ease
and open our eyes to find you, God with us
in this day's feasting and tomorrow's rest
and each day's unexpected joy or pain.

For there is so much to see this Christmas night:
still in the winter dark the stars are singing
and we have heard the words of angels
(for the Monarch has spoken)
Glory to God in the Highest
and Peace on Earth
in a baby's cry –
and far away
a cross is lifted on a distant hill.

Heather Pencavel

Christmas Meditation

In the night
Hid from sight
Coming silently the world's true light

In winter cold
As prophets told
Comes the son of God brave and bold

162

In his mother's womb
To the unfurnished room
His destiny the cross and tomb.

All was silent that winter's night
No light shone through the piercing cold
The shepherds stamped their frozen feet
Travellers wound their icy way
And the good folk slept in dreamless beds
As all the world lay cold and dead.

Who would have dreamt in a peasant's womb
In a hidden room where no light came
Where all was poor and quite unknown
And dark and cold lay down to sleep
That the source of time would come to birth
That love was coming down to earth?

In the night
Hid from sight
Coming silently the world's true light

In winter cold
As prophets told
Comes the son of God brave and bold

In his mother's womb
To the unfurnished room
His destiny the cross and tomb.

James Ashdown

A Gift of Peace

Leader: May the love that breathes life into all humanity
and all of creation

All: **Be born in us tonight/today**

Leader: May the love that brings us healing

All: **Be born in us tonight/today**

Leader: May the love that overcomes hatred

All: **Be born in us tonight/today**

Leader: May the love that forgives and renews

All: **Be born in us tonight/today**

Leader: May the love that brings the blessing of peace

All: **Be born in us tonight/today**

Leader: May that Peace now be the gift we share with each other

Richard Becher

A Christmas Baby

'I am looking for God. Where is He?' asked the little girl.

But the Philosopher's words were too difficult for he said:

Scan the world.
You will not observe Him whom you seek.
He is called 'One not seen'.

Listen to all things.
You will not hear Him whom you seek.
He is called 'The Silent One'.

Seize what is there.
You will not grasp Him whom you seek.
He is called 'One untouched'.

But a mother smiled. Taking the child in her arms, she parted
the straw and showed her the new-born baby.

Derek Webster

If Only . . .

If the stable was my body,
in which my heart was a manger
from where love cried out,
Jesus would be born again
and transform God's world today.

Richard Becher

Cradled-Christ Eucharist

God reached out
and
with the lightest
of touch,
set the world aflame
with his adoration.

He so loved
each
and every one,
that he gave
his most Beloved Son
in order that we,
that is
you
and me
and all humankind,
might be born anew.

Not only on Earth,
but
in Heaven, too,
and cascading
through all of Creation,
is the cradled-Christ Eucharist.

Susan Hardwick

He's Grown, That Baby

He's grown, that Baby.
Not that most people have noticed.
He still looks the same,
Lying there in the straw, with
Animals and shepherds looking on.
He's safe there, locked in that moment
Where time met Eternity.

Reality of course is different,
He grew up, astonished people with his
Insight, disturbed them with
Ideas that stretched them into
New maturity.

Some found him
Much too difficult to cope with,
Nailed him down to fit their
Narrow minds.

We are more subtle,
Keep him helpless,
Refuse to let him be the Man he is,
Adore him as the Christmas Baby,
Eternally unable to grow up
Until we set him free.

By all means let us pause there
At the stable, and
Marvel at the miracle of birth.
But we'll never get to know
God with us, until we learn
To find him at the Inn,
A fellow guest who shares the joy and sorrow,
The host who is the life we celebrate.

He's grown, that Baby.

Ann Lewin

The Family of Christ
Tempting Providence

First World.
Third World.
Who on earth was it who
tempted Providence
by sound-biting such words as these?

They clearly did not remember
What it was that Jesus said:
'The first shall be last
and the last shall be first
at my Christmas feast.'

Susan Hardwick

For the Rich and the Poor

For the rich and the poor
Jesus came for both on Christmas Day
Unto them he was born in a stable
No fame or honour was attached to his birth
In a common family he made his appearance

For the rich and the poor
He made his presence felt by both classes
The uneducated and the learned paid him homage
The shepherds left their flocks and went to see him
Three kings from the East presented him with precious gifts

For the rich and the poor
He came though earthly rulers of the day were upset
Let alone the most feared religious leaders
Even to such the Saviour of the world was born
Others were filled with joy whilst some with bitterness

For the 'haves' and the 'have-nots'
Jesus came to identify with them
As he had no comfortable pillow in the stable
So he is in solidarity with the refugees and homeless
For the exploited and the suffering children he came

For the rich and the poor
He came to save them from the sins of the world
As his coming culminated in his death on the cross
He offered his life for the salvation of the entire human race
Let us thank God for giving us his one and only Son.

Goodwin Zainga
Malawi

A Sort of Bethlehem

Feelings, words, cross themselves,
commit themselves to their journey,
convey themselves across kingdoms,
meet a sympathetic response,
settle down to lodge in fond thoughts,
come in out of the cold,
see joy turn gestation and labour
into the womb's fruit that leaps, gasps,

seizes on breath, takes grip on our fingers,
embraces straw heaped for a stranger,
curls crib, pillow and last resting place,
under the heart, held close to the breast –
throb of the mother-responder.
So a few feelings, words,
sent away under the stars, across water,
find the soft landing
that empathy has prepared for them,
a new-born child, an unexpected letter,
a sort of Bethlehem:
a gift freely given, gratefully received,
that blows bubbles across the spheres.

Brian Louis Pearce

Holy Innocents

Why Them?

Holy Innocents: 28 December
Matthew 2:13–18

God, you must weep to see
The massacre of different
Innocents.
Stick limbs on swollen bellies,
Faces old before their time,
Skin stretched on grinning skulls.

We sit before the screen
And watch them die;
And from the world,
Mingling with your tears,
Comes Rachel's anguished cry
Because they are not.

And we could have helped.

Ann Lewin

Herod's High and Mighty Stand

Herod's high and mighty stand
Showed the power at his command,
Slaughtered children in the land:

Kyrie, Lord have mercy,
Kyrie, Lord have mercy,
Kyrie, Lord have mercy on us.

170

Mary wept, she understood,
Wept as every mother should,
Ramah's echo, death to good:

Surely force has had its day,
Brutish whim and power's display;
Yet our actions truth betray:

Seen on every paper's page,
Words of hate and fists of rage,
Sings of greed in every age:

Anger still inflicts the pain,
Each excuse is seen as lame,
Yet again we bear the shame:

Till through this and every time
people cease from heinous crime,
Till with peace their actions rhyme:

Tune: 7.7.7 metre

Andrew Pratt

Was There No Other Way?

I shall recount the Lord's unfailing love (Isaiah 63:7)

Because he himself has passed through the test of suffering, he is able to help those who are in the midst of their test (Hebrews 2:18)

When Herod realised that the astrologers had tricked him he flew into a rage, and gave orders for the massacre of all the boys aged two years or under, in Bethlehem and throughout the whole district (Matthew 2:16)

The Christ Child
is saved from Herod's wrath,
God's purposes have not been thwarted;
but – at what a price!
Our hearts go out to the families
whose children were slaughtered.
They had no warning,
no means of escape.
Did this really have to be?
Was there no other way?

> Even as we praise you, Lord,
> we cannot escape the darker side of life.
> Is it right that we should be rejoicing
> in blessings received
> while others are engulfed in tragedy?
> We find it hard to understand
> the suffering so many have to endure.
> We hold to the fact that in Jesus
> you identified yourself with the weak,
> the helpless,
> and with all who endure pain or sorrow.
> We still cannot understand
> why the world is the way it is,
> but we do believe that you are calling us
> to play our part in carrying on the work of Jesus.
> Stiffen our resolve, we pray,
> to give help in his name
> wherever we have the opportunity to do so.

Edmund Banyard

The Suleiman Family

The Suleimans are a Christian Palestinian family living on the
outskirts of Bethlehem, in the Occupied Territories. Samir, the
father, is unemployed; Maha, the mother, is a housewife.

Their two children, Najwa, aged ten and her brother Naim, aged sixteen, have grown up in Bethlehem. They have progressed well at school but the school has been closed many times and their education has been disrupted. There has been conflict between the Israelis and the Palestinians throughout their lives.

At Christmas they feel privileged to live in Bethlehem. Curfews and other rules set by the Israelis limit what they can do. Like many other Palestinian families they choose to celebrate Christmas in a limited way. They feel that they cannot celebrate the birth of Jesus Christ, the Prince of Peace, until there is peace in their land. At Christmas, they join with Christians around the world in prayers for peace.

They have not given up hope.

Christian Aid

Pray for Peace

'I want to ask you to keep praying. The more you pray for peace among Palestinians and Israelis, the more we feel we are not alone.'

Bishop Samir Kafity
Christian Aid

Our Lady of the Refugees

Mother, who heard the child whimper
Beneath the thin blue shawl,
Our aching hearts cry out to thee;
Mother, pray for them all.

A thousand Bethlehems mask dark tonight,
The eyes of little friendly homes have lost their light.
Pathetic heaps of poor, dead things are laid aside . . .

173

A latched door swings,
A small bird sings.

Mother, whose sad Egyptian flight preceded all of these,
Guide them in faith beneath familiar stars
Our Lady of the Refugees.

Source Unknown

Harassed, Haunted Child of Mary

Harassed, haunted child of Mary
Ran before he learned to crawl;
Filled with horror, those who loved him
Those who gave to him their all,
Tore him from his bed and birth place,
Exiled fearing more than thrall.

Doubt and danger dogged each footfall,
Normal sounds now raised their fear;
Noises in a cobbled courtyard:
Herod's minions drawing near?
Or the waking sounds of morning?
Nothing now is safe or clear.

Out of this endangered childhood,
Rootless, no asylum found,
Grew the strength of God to greatness,
Yet with thorns his brow was crowned:
Clothes divided, scourged, derided,
Suffering without a sound.

Dare we beautify the image
When his heirs still walk this earth,
When our children, harassed, hounded,
Suffer death before their birth,

While their parents' haunted hunger
Speaks of their discarded worth?

Tune: 8.7.8.7.8.7 metre

Andrew Pratt

Christ our God

The debt burden is killing people because people cannot afford to go to the hospital. If they don't have drugs, they die. It is a direct result of the debt crisis.

Canon H. P. Mtingele,
General Secretary of the Church of the Province of Tanzania

Christ our God,
you too were born a child
not free into our world:
subject to poverty,
harassment by foreign powers,
and dangers to your health.
In your name
let us cry freedom for your children
now, at this time,
and through all generations.

Janet Morley, Hannah Ward, Jennifer Wild
Christian Aid

Nativity Now

This presentation involves:

- *a maximum of six readers but only one or two need to be involved*
- *a man and a woman – with a real baby, if possible*
- *one or two people to represent each of the different groups mentioned in the narrative*
- *a few simple props which people representing the different groups wear/hold*
- *a large but very simple wooden cross*

175

Great Advantage: No-one has to learn any words!

The couple with baby walk slowly to the front of (the church).
She sits facing front and he stands behind her.

Reader: Here are two people –
a man and a woman –
just as at Bethlehem,
sharing their lives together,
loving and caring for each other,
whose child is born,
with rejoicing and hope
and faith in the future –
born into a world full of confusion,
insecurity and danger . . .
Born into a world
which God cherishes
and wants to reclaim.

Representatives of these people walk forward and stand
round the couple.

Reader: Here are the every-day people –
manual workers, on factory assembly lines,
who clock in and out in a daily routine.
Civil servants and shop assistants,
programmers and tele-sales operatives,
students and traffic wardens,
whose lives are filled with comings and goings;
and who find it hard to hear the Good News
above the roar of the traffic
and the jangle of mobile phones;
or to believe in the reality of God
in a self-absorbed society.

Yet for whom the stable door stands open,
and the Word remains accessible
to all who search for it.

Representatives of these people (one might be wearing chains) walk forward and stand around the couple.

Reader: Here are the dispossessed of the world,
the outcasts and the unwelcome –
whose faces seem strange,
who speak in different languages, and belong to
   alien cultures.
The imprisoned and forgotten people,
and those who beg
on the street corners of the world.
The lost and the lonely,
the uninvited guests,
who find a welcome at the birthplace
of a vulnerable God.

Representatives of these people come forward and stand around the couple.

Reader: Here are the rulers of our generation;
the presidents and prime ministers,
the multi-national company executives,
the oil magnates and arms dealers,
the research scientists and IT consultants –
some coming in humility
to bring gifts to their Lord,
but some, in their arrogance,
offering only the gold of corruption,
the incense of warfare,
and the myrrh of betrayal.

Some of the group raise the cross above the heads of the couple.

Reader: Here is the cross.
The gift that we gave
when the child became man,
and refused to conform
to ritual and rite.
Who offered forgiveness
to all who believed him
and stretched out his arms
in a salvation's embrace.

Addressed to the congregation – during which the group disperses.

Reader: And here are the people
who have heard the Good News
who say 'Yes' to God and follow his call.
Who celebrate with joy
the mystery of the incarnation –
and go out to human encounter
in the power and love of God,
which even the darkness of death
can never destroy.

Jill Jenkins

A Carol for Roshita

Roshita was born on 1 March 2000, in a tree where her mother had climbed for safety when her home was destroyed by floods in Mozambique.

When Jesus was born in Bethlehem
his mother found nowhere to stay
apart from the cave at the back of the inn,
the cave where animals lay.

When I was born in Mozambique
my mother had lost her home.

It was swept away in the terrible floods,
   the torrents of whirlpool and foam.

Heavy and weary, she climbed a tree.
For three nights she stayed awake
and kept her hold on a rainswept branch.
   She said it was for my sake.

When Jesus was born in Bethlehem
a star moved across the sky
and angels appeared to the shepherds at night
   singing 'Glory to God on high.'

When I was born in Mozambique
an airman stretched out his arm
and took me, and wrapped me in strips of cloth,
   and lifted me clear from harm.

They say Jesus Christ is the Son of God
but I think he's rather like me.
For Jesus was born in a cattle trough
and I was born in a tree.

Barbara Moss

It Is Dark Outside and Very Cold

Voice One: It is dark outside and very cold.
          When Jesus was born it was dark and cold too.

Voice Two: Winter in Bethlehem is chilly, wet
          with frost in the desert
          and snow on Mount Hermon
          and worse still there was the cold power
          of the Romans
          holding down people with heavy taxes
          and swashbuckling swords.

179

Voice One: Jesus was born in a dangerous world
filled with disease and early death
filled with riots and crucifixions.

Voice Two: But he came with Good News.
God cares about people in tough times.

God has hope for the world.
Tonight we care,
celebrating that Good News.
So . . .

Voice One: *   Sing till sundown, hum your joy,
dress in starlight, girl and boy.
Man and woman climb the hill,
warmed beyond December's chill,
reeling, clapping, touch the air,
is that fragrant music there?

Voice Two: *   Come the glory, gone the gloom:
in a wondrous huddled room.
Christ the Word we've longed to know
calls us dancing through the snow

* *Verse one of the hymn 'Sing till Sundown'*
  The second verse appears below

Oriole and Art Veldhuis
-30C Winnipeg Canada

Sing till Sundown

Verse Two

Gladness deepens into grace,
weaves its light on every face.
Let us wake the sleeping earth,
celebrate the sweetest birth,

pierce the night with festive cry,
bloom in colours of the sky.
Bring the flute, the tambourine,
wave the branch of evergreen.
Lost we were a grief ago,
now we're dancing through the snow.

Eileen Spinelli
USA

A Time for Welcoming the Prince of Peace

These were the streets we walked as pilgrims,
passing by the market stalls and praying at the stations of
the cross.
Here was the wall of wailing where past destruction was
remembered
and here the reading of a million names of children
murdered
and a thousand candle lights to pierce the darkness in
remembrance.
Yet in this same city now the noise of guns and bombs.
How can Jerusalem welcome the Prince of Peace?

Here are the shepherds' fields we visited,
a place where even now we seem to hear the angel's
message,
where the little town is busy with its visitors
and Manger Square is thronged with people
who make their way to the place of nativity.
Yet here too are armed soldiers and cries of hate.
How can Bethlehem welcome the Child of Peace?

Here in Nazareth the streets are busy down below
and settlements are sturdily built on the hills above.
There is water in the well where Mary heard the message
and it seems that even now you can hear the angel's voice.

181

Yet Nazareth too has become a place of tension
and fear stalks the streets where the holy family lived.
How can Nazareth welcome the Child of Love?

The answer lies in reconciliation
and the true heart of religion's message.
When God himself comes down amongst us,
then enmity is overcome and hate turned to love,
then the oppressed are lifted high and the poor are given
    hope,
for this is the time of magnificat
and we too give joy-filled praise to the God of Peace.

John Johansen-Berg

God, Born as a Baby

God, born as a baby,
we pray for children who cry and are not comforted;
for those who live and die
without a roof, without bread, without protection.

God, for whom there was no room at the inn,
we pray for those who are denied shelter;
for those who struggle against cold and damp and hunger
and those searching for a place of security.

God, forced to flee from the wrath of Herod,
we pray for those uprooted by tyranny;
for those fleeing from violence
and for those seeking safety in places strange to them.

God, whose coming was announced with words of peace,
we pray for a world in the shadow of war;
for those who have already lost homes and livelihood
and those who fear for their own survival.

God, coming to us,
help us to meet you in the poor and unprotected;
and to greet you with the Christmas hope of peace and
    freedom
singing in our hearts.

Jan Berry

Celebrating Christmas

Celebrating Christmas: turkey, mince-pies, crackers,
presents and cards, family and friends, wine and chocolates,
carols and midnight services, toys and games for the children.
A celebration of the birth of One whose name is
Wonderful Counsellor, Mighty God,
Everlasting Father, Prince of Peace,
who comes to establish justice and righteousness for ever.

Hundreds of asylum seekers spent Christmas in detention.
In purpose-built detention centres, perhaps –
their number is on the increase –
or old Victorian buildings long past their 'best before' date,
with echoing metal walkways and safety nets between floors,
and heavy metal doors which crash open and clang shut
    again.
Nothing to do but read – but the books are mostly in English –
or play snooker, or cards, or think desperate thoughts.

Prince of Peace, war-torn countries cry out for you,
Mighty God, where states abuse their own citizens, establish
    justice,
Wonderful Counsellor, be a guide to the lost and bewildered.

And, Lord, I want to share in your work.
Help me to find out what you want me to do.

Louise Pirouet

Sometimes I Cry

Sometimes I cry when I think of the child
born in a stable, no room anywhere
growing to live in a world cold with grief and shame
dying in agony, nailed there by fear.

Sometimes I pray when I think of the child
born to be human in weakness and care,
growing to stand with the poor and the prisoner
dying to raise them in freedom to share.

Sometimes I laugh when I think of the child
born without name on the edge of the town
growing in powerlessness, changer of images,
dying derided and mocked as a clown.

Sometimes I tremble when I think of the child
born out of mystery, starlight and sign,
maker of miracles out of reality,
raising them up till the end of time.

But sometimes I sing when I think of the child
born out of joy and obedience and pain,
growing to touch human living with ecstasy
dying to show us that love lives again.

Kathy Galloway
Scotland

The Child is Missing

First Sunday after Christmas Day

I Samuel 2:18–20, 26 and Luke 2:41–52

*The child is missing – a moment's inattention, then
the lurch of the heart, the sinking of the stomach
'I thought he was with you.'*

184

The child is missing – the ache of longing, even after years
even when you know he is safe, even when there are other children,
'I wonder what he's doing now?'

The child is missing – wandering the streets without a home:
home is where blows are struck, and darkness brings abuse and now
'She's gone – good riddance!'

The child is missing – he slept last night in this shop doorway
till they came with guns, street cleansing, and he died.
'They got Carlos – tonight it might be us.'

Parent God
Hannah knew where Samuel was, and missed him.
Mary and Joseph found Jesus in the end,
safe in the Temple learning
(as well as all the teachers' knowledge)
what agony of fear his parents feel,
how much they love him.

Children disappear every day
and are not always found
though they are often missed.
We pray for all missing children and their parents:
children kidnapped and afraid,
the runaways, the disappeared,
children given for adoption.
Teach us how to build homes where everyone is valued
communities where everyone is safe
and a world where all children are able to grow
strong in mind and body
as Jesus did.

Heather Pencavel

A Prayer for All Holy Innocents

O God, deliver our world
from the recurring conflicts
that close borders,
close schools,
close minds,
and shut off the future
Give the children freedom
to learn from their heritage,
read their own language,
and take pride in their people.

Janet Morley
Christian Aid

Christmas Worship

Christmas Songs

Let's Go to Bethlehem

Soldiers march, to the town, with the sound
of joyful singing all around;
in our minds, let our eyes seek the light
of Bethlehem.

Light a candle to welcome him,
Christ the Lord, our eternal King,
This is good news for everyone –
Our Saviour's come.

Far and wide, day and night, people strive,
their place of birth they long to find;
to this view, we shall too journey through
to Bethlehem.

Light a candle to welcome him . . .

Weary eyes, Mary sighs, feeling tired,
poor Joseph stumbles on beside,
to the place, God displays love's embrace
through his dear Son.

Light a candle to welcome him . . .

Shephers come, see them run, hear their song
all down the road to Bethlehem;
joyfully, we can sing, praise the King
of Bethlehem.

Light a candle to welcome him . . .

Tune: Zither Carol

Peter Ratcliffe/Jubilate Hymns

The Blackthorn Carol

The night was so cold, on the snowline of winter.
Where sheep huddled soft in the grey light of dawn;
When dazzling the darkness the heavens blazed round us,
Bright angels proclaiming a Saviour was born.

So come, leave the flock, wait no longer in wonder,
Run ragged and rough-shod to Bethlehem town,
Though the poor of the world have no bounty to offer
From the buds of the blackthorn we'll weave him a crown.

This child, who lies sleeping so quiet in his cradle,
Will house with the humble and walk with the wise;
Will teach of his kingdom, where pride has no portion,
Touch lepers, mend madness and lighten blind eyes.

When envy and weakness betray and condemn him,
From lashes of loathing his blood will run down;
When broken he hangs on the cross of conviction,
From the barbs of the blackthorn we'll weave him a crown.

When women walk weeping with spices to salve him,
While morning is drawing its first shining breath –
His tomb will be empty, his grave-clothes discarded,
As love leaps to life from the dungeon of death.

When all is accomplished, creation completed,
To the high king of heaven the world will bow down,
When the tree of all knowledge bears fruits of forgiveness,
From the blossoms of blackthorn we'll weave him a crown.

Tune: The Streets of Laredo/The Bard of Armagh

Jill Jenkins

Christmas in the Southern Hemisphere

Christmas in the summer?
Heat instead of cold?
Flowers instead of freezing?
Skies that shine like gold?
This is Southern Christmas,
Seasons in reverse!
Can the Northern pictures
Speak in Southern verse?

Inner space is timeless –
God is everywhere –
Cries of newborn infants
Reach for Mary's care.
When we nurture wonder
'Till its grace abounds
We create new pictures
Outside Northern bounds.

Sing the Christmas story –
Carol South and North –
Sing of pregnant seasons,
Nature's songs of birth.
Raise the Christchild's praises –
Lift both joy and pain –
Touch the realms of oneness –
Live the birth again.

Tune: Cranham

W. L. Wallace
Aotearoa New Zealand

What Star Shall We Follow?

How ancient and lovely this news of a star,
a baby, a mother, the kings from afar.
Come close now, Lord Jesus, we ask you to stay
And show us your face in your people today.

What star shall we follow but one that leads here
to a baby born homeless and a family in fear?
What heaven shall we long for but one that starts there
for all the world's children in your tender care?

We thank you, Lord Jesus, for coming to earth;
for the light in the darkness that shone at your birth,
for life in its fullness that you promise today,
and the hope in a baby asleep on the hay.

Tune: Away in a Manger

Rebecca Dudley
Christian Aid

Christmas Prayers

A Prayer of Confession for Christmas Eve

Luke 2:15–20

No place for him;
there was no place for him.

Forgive us, God,
that even tonight
children are being born
for whom there is no place:
whose lives are blighted from the beginning,
through lack of love,
lack of nourishment,
lack of shelter.

Forgive us that too often
there is no place
in our lives
for the Son of your love
who came to make peace and justice possible.

Let him be born again in us tonight
and find a warm place in our hearts,
so that the truth and hope,
the joy and peace he brings
may not be homeless
but find an abiding place
in our lives,
and the lives of the nations.

He comes with forgiveness;
he comes with healing;
he comes with faith, hope and love:
he comes to be at home with us
for ever.

Alan Gaunt

A Prayer for Christmas Eve (1)

Out of the darkness
we listen for the cry
a cry of praise above despair; *
of life beyond death:
the mother's bearing cry: *
the cry of pain transformed to joy.

We listen for the cry
of the newly born,
coming out of darkness into light,
the cry of infinite tender frailty, *
which tells us that God is with us.

Here is love which excels all treasures.

This, above all,
is what we long for in our hearts;
bringing hope from despair;
joy from sorrow;
peace from turmoil.

Here is love that runs deeper than all time's wrong,
to save the earth
from terror,
torture,
doubt and tumult.

Without your birth,
Lord Jesus Christ,
how vain earth's mornings are! *

But now you come
to liberate our hearts,
to cleanse our minds of all bitterness,
to fill our souls with eternal peace,
and to carry us away
from old fears and disenchantments.

You are hope for us,
you are joy for us,
you are peace for us,
tonight and for evermore.

Alan Gaunt

* These phrases are taken or adapted
from poems by Vernon Watkins.

A Prayer for Christmas Eve (2)

Eternal God,
let the wonder of childhood,
be the wonder, still,
of faith and maturity.
May we never be so wise,
as to lose the wisdom of innocence.

May we never be so self-sure
as to lose the power of helpless love.

Let it be as true for us tonight,
as it has ever been,
that a Saviour is born for us,
born in Bethlehem of our poor hearts,
who is the Prince of peace.

We come to remember him:
to remember what he was on earth,
a baby, one of millions, born to die,
and yet your presence with us,
full of holy love.

And we remember that now,
he is for ever human with us,
pleading for the end of pain and evil,
for the time when none will hurt and none destroy:
when flesh will not be broken any more by human means,
and blood will not be shed.

For this he was born, for this he died,
and this he will accomplish in us.
And so we pray,
that on this night of all the year,
we may realise your holy Spirit present with us,
the source of deep merriment;
making us the living signs
of the wonder of Christmas,
fulfilled through Good Friday,
Easter and Pentecost.

So it is, tonight,
we join in the thanksgiving and praise,
which has been offered to you for two thousand years,
by Christians without number;
the thanksgiving and praise
which has been offered to you
since the dawn of human time;
the thanksgiving and praise
which is offered to you eternally.

Alan Gaunt

A Christmas Prayer for Peace

We pray to the almighty God,
great shepherd of the flocks,
for peace in the land where Jesus was born;
for peace wherever there is conflict;
for peace in our homes and our families,
so that all may go their ways with justice and security,
and dance where soldiers marched.

Christian Aid

A Christmas Prayer of Confession

God of stable, stars and surprises,
of light and hope and new life:
open our eyes and hearts to your presence in our world;
forgive our obsession with property and possessions;
forgive our compromises and narrowness of vision.
Open us to your grace,
that we might hear again the song of the angels,
and respond with a song in our hearts,
and in our lives.
Amen.

Gordon Nodwell
Canada

Prayers of Intercession (1)

Our world, this Christmas morning,
has moved a long way from the traditional setting
of shepherds on a hillside, astrologers from a distant land,
a young girl and an old man seeking shelter,
the cry of a newborn child tearing the night air . . .

We live in an urban society,
we work in warm offices or shops or schools or factories

195

and our food comes from the supermarket.
We travel by car or plane and telephone to say we're coming
and arrange accommodation in advance –
unless we're homeless and hungry and have no welfare rights
and no way of getting work.

We fill in tax forms
and register for health care and education –
no need to return to the place of our birth –
unless we're black and they don't want us here,
and they won't let us through Immigration Control.
A stable where you're welcome is better
than an airport where you'll probably be sent away.

Our babies are born decently in clinical surroundings
with pink and blue cards and hand-knitted bootees –
unless we live in Africa, in which case
they'll probably die before they're five anyway
but not before we've learnt to love and suffer with them
and their feeble wails tear at our nerve-ends.

Our world this Christmas Day is full of pain
and its problems are more than we can bear.
Our Happy Christmas only makes things worse
mocking poverty with our plastic purchases,
and the pain will not go away.

We hold the world and its pain before you, hurting and
    healing God,
for it is into this world that you are born
and it is not only our world but yours.
We pray for our world – yours and ours – in hope.
In quietness now we offer to you
all those who need our prayers . . .

We thank you that the light shines on in the darkness
and the darkness has never overcome it.

Help us who follow the child whose light shone in a dark
    stable
to be light for others this Christmas Day
and every day.

Heather Pencavel

Prayers of Intercession (2)

God
you could have come
with miracle and magic
in a flash of light
in a hurricane of judgement
so that the earth shook
and the universe trembled

but you chose to come
in a baby's newborn cry
you chose to make your coming known
to working men on a cold hillside
to wandering scholars
to an innkeeper
and to the beasts of the field.

Because you came, a baby,
born to a young girl
you brought miracle and magic and mystery
into ordinary things
and the whole creation sings at your coming
and is blessed.

*

God of love, Child in the manger, you are here
in all the excitement and delight of this Christmas morning
we recognise you,

in the love that has prepared our gifts
in the wonder of small children
in the gladness of family reunions
in the patience and care for young and old
in the retelling of the story of the baby
the account of the moment in history
when God was embraced by humankind.
We thank you for this mystery
that in Jesus, Immanuel, God is with us.

God of love, who travelled into Egypt for fear of Herod,
you are here
in all the suffering and sadness which are still real this
Christmas morning
we recognise you,
in the people who are on the run from danger and oppression
who wake up today in airport lounges or immigration centres
among strangers, far away from home
and in all people who have nowhere to sleep tonight.
We pray for them and ask that you will show us
how to build a world that welcomes strangers
and finds in them the God who is with us.

God of peace, who lay asleep in a woman's arms,
born into an occupied land, you are here
we recognise you,
a child asleep, powerless and in danger
in every place where there is tension and unrest
conflict and violence.
We pray for all who suffer from the effects of conflict
either in their homes or in their communities or nations,
and for all who work to make peace between people
or between governments. Show us how to build a society
which values the safety of the sleeping child
and helps him to grow up in peace
in a community of justice.

We thank you that two thousand years after the story of Jesus
God is still with us. And God promises us
that in Jesus God fills our whole life
and our whole world
until at last
everyone will share in the wonder and delight
of the love that comes at Christmas.

Heather Pencavel

Prayers Around a Nativity Scene

Leader: As we look on the shepherds,
we pray for people who work through the night
    while others sleep,
who have to stay awake for long hours,
receive low wages and are little respected.

All: **We pray for all women and men on night shifts.**

Leader: As we look on the wise men,
we pray for people who question the world
until they get the truth,
who are ready to take risky journeys
and go different ways to get home.

All: **We pray for women and men who journey in faith.**

Leader: As we look on the nativity scene,
we think of the forces that gathered in the darkness
    outside;
we pray for the soldiers who have orders to kill,
and for those who give them their orders.

All: **We pray for the weak – and the powerful – who
are afraid.**

Leader: As we look on the angels,
we pray for the people who bring good news of
peace,
who startle us with the chance that brings change.
We pray for messengers of hope.

All: **And this will be a sign for us . . . a child lying in
a manger.**

Christian Aid

Let there be Light

Leader: Let us pray:

This Christmas, as we remember the birth of Jesus
in a stable,
we are reminded that hope comes in unexpected
ways
and in unfamiliar places.
We pray for the work of schools in . . . *(name
countries)*

Wherever the world is in darkness, Lord,

All: **Let there be light.**

Leader: This Christmas, as we remember the violence with
which the soldiers came searching for Jesus,
we are reminded that conflicts still have devastating
effects on children trapped between warring
sides.
We pray for conflict zones and look for peace.
(name current situations where there are conflicts)

Wherever the world is in darkness, Lord,

All: **Let there be light.**

Leader: This Christmas, as we remember the flight of Jesus'
family to Egypt,
we are reminded of the plight of people forced to
flee from homes and possessions.
We pray for refugees and asylum seekers. *(name the
countries)*

Wherever the world is in darkness, Lord,

All: **Let there be light.**

Leader: This Christmas, as we remember the homeless
Holy Family,
we are reminded of the millions of families now
who have no shelter and who face eviction.
We pray for all homeless people wherever they are
in the world. *(name people known to you in your
community and in the wider global situations)*

Wherever the world is in darkness, Lord,

All: **Let there be light.**

Leader: This Christmas, as we remember those who went
to the stable,
we are reminded that we need to make a journey.
We pray for ourselves that as you have come to us,
we may also come to know you,
to know you and to love you more
as we serve other people.

Wherever the world is in darkness, Lord,

All: **Let there be light.**

Christian Aid

An Intercessory Meditation

The silence of the night
  can be long and lonely
  with no-one at your side
  to speak a friendly word
  or share a prayer of hope.
The silence of the night
  for people on their own
  with no hand to hold
  and no smiling face to behold
  is such a lonely place.
So we pray for today's
  lonely people
  hidden in the darkness
  but needing your embrace
  to strengthen and heal.
May your love break through
the silence of the night.

Sung response: Tune: Stille Nacht (Silent Night)

Jesus Christ, Prince of Peace
Son of God, come tonight
like a shining light of hope
bringing heavenly peace to earth
with your healing love,
with your healing love.

Some nights are not so silent
  for bombs disturb the peace
  and people cry for help
  in the darkness of the night
  as needless lives are lost.
Some nights are not so silent
  for the homeless refugee
  forced to keep on moving,

202

bullied to submission,
losing all possessions.
So we pray tonight
for those who dream of silence
to disturb the sound of war
which screams above the peace
with rockets, bombs and bullets
and brings a devil's death
instead of Christ's new life.

Pause for quiet

May your love break through
the silence of the night.

Sung response

Every night is a Holy night
for God of heaven and earth
as the Spirit moves among us,
touching people's lives,
speaking through the silence
and healing many wounds.
Every night is a Holy night
for those with faith in God
who hears our every prayer
and shares the pain we feel.
So we bring to the silence
our prayers for those we know
who need a healing touch
in the quietness of a Holy night.

Pause for quiet

May your love break through
the silence of the night.

> Not many nights are silent,
>> but every night is Holy
>> for God made day and night,
>> separating light from dark
>> and in Christ we find
>> the light of truth
>> to lead us through the dark
>> and meet again with God,
>> forgiven, healed, renewed.
> So if your nights are silent
>> let them be also Holy
>> as you listen for God
>> whose Spirit came upon a child
>> and turned His word to flesh
>> so we may find new life today.

Pause for quiet

> May your love break through
> the silence of the night.

Sung response

> The sung response can be used to words of a different prayer and at other
> times of the year.

Richard Becher

A Christmas Prayer

As once you came in the hush of darkness, O God,
so still our hearts now
by the wonder of this night.
Make us wise with the wisdom of a little one,
that truth might be born afresh in us.

Let not our hearts be busy inns with no room,
but doors opened wide to welcome a Holy Guest,
who is Jesus Christ, alive with you and the Holy Spirit,
one God, now and for ever.
Amen.

Robert Stark
Canada

Prayers Reflecting on Christmas

God of love you come to earth
wherever a baby's first cry
shatters the air

you speak when a child says its first word
you grow and laugh and play
in the fun and excitement of growing up
you question and challenge
in the teenager's struggle for identity and understanding

you share the pleasure of work well done
the joy of achievement
the fulfilment of learning
the breath-taking fear of new adventures
the delight of success

your love is our love
when it reaches out to another person
mother and son
father and daughter
lover, husband and wife
the weak, the old, the vulnerable
homeless and starving ones
refugee and alien

205

your pain is our pain
weakness and frustration
powerlessness and oppression
the darkness of death
all these are both ours and yours

because you came, God with us,
one of us
a baby
a child
a boy
a man
a mortal

the man Christ Jesus
the Child Immanuel
God with us

We worship and adore you
every day we live, through Jesus Christ, your Son, our
   Saviour.
Amen.

Heather Pencavel

Wonderful Counsellor

Wonderful Counsellor, give your wisdom to the rulers of the
   nations.
Mighty God, make the whole world know that the
   government is on your shoulders.
Everlasting Father, establish your reign of justice and
   righteousness for ever.
Prince of Peace, bring in the endless kingdom of your peace.
Almighty Lord, hear our prayer and fulfil your purposes in
   us, as you accomplished your will in our Lord Jesus Christ.
Amen

The Promise of His Glory

A Christmas Eucharist

A Christmas Communion Liturgy

Invitation and Offering:

Bethlehem is a long way away,
and Jesus was born a long time ago.

But Jesus was born for us,
He is here with us still.

Jesus invites us
to meet him at this table.

**As Shepherds came to the stable
to celebrate the birth of a Saviour,
we come to worship.**

All who come in fear
        or in need,
all who come in wonder
        or in hope,
all who come in love
        and in joy,
are welcome here.

**As we come, we bring to the table
symbols of our lives offered in thanks.
Here is bread.
Here is wine.
Here is money.**

As wise men brought gifts
to praise a new King,
these are our gifts
offered in adoration and praise.

Thanksgiving:

God of all goodness
We thank you for the Word made flesh among us,
for the birth of Jesus Christ our Lord;
for his coming as the
least among the least,
in poverty among the poor.
In vulnerability and need
you have placed your love at our disposal,
becoming for us a living hope
in the midst of our powerlessness;
challenging the proud
and overcoming the powers
that oppress and enslave us.

With thanksgiving we remember
Mary's loving response to your purpose,
Joseph's care-full obedience to your will,
and we remember all who have responded
to grace by offering their lives
to make incarnate the promise of your justice
and now share the fullness of your joy.
For us and for all
for the ones who struggle and suffer
and long for freedom and peace,
Jesus on the night of his arrest
took bread, and wine
and shared them,
saying:
'This is my Body' –
broken for all who are broken,

'This is my Blood' –
shed for all who bleed.

So we celebrate Jesus' birth
and give thanks for his life,
his death on the cross,
his resurrection and ascension:

With angel choirs,
With ordinary shepherds,
With the wise ones,
With all God's people,
We lift our hearts in joyful praise.

Touched by the Spirit,
in bread and wine,
make us one body
with Christ in suffering and glory.
Together in him
we will praise you,
and serve you in the world
until the gift of Christmas is fulfilled
for us and for all creation.
Amen

Sharing of Bread and Wine

Prayer after Communion:

Glory to God in the highest heaven
And on earth peace to those with whom he is pleased.

God, Giver of joy,
we thank you for meeting us here
in the child born to save us.
You have prepared us for our journey.

The light of Christ, shining like a star,
shows us the way we should go,
and the ones we should serve.
May our faces, lifted up in wonder and expectation,
reflect that light for all who live in darkness.
Amen

Peter Trow

A Post Communion Prayer
for Christmas Eve or Christmas Day

Lord Jesus Christ
in the immensity of your innocence
be born in us tonight.

We have come with joy and sorrow,
with delight and anxiety,
for the world,
for people we love
and ourselves.

We are here
because this is Christmas
and there is expectation in the air,
as we recall again
the child who was born for us
who is peace for the world.

Eternal God,
in the name of Jesus we pray
for all humankind:
strong and weak,
poor and rich,
tyrants and tyrannised:
that they may kneel at the manger,
seeking help and healing.

Great God,
all sufficient for us,
like a mother with her new-born child:
we praise you for the coming
of your uniquely precious One: Jesus
to be our shining star!
We praise you for all who hear his laughter
through the silence
and make their way through sorrow
to his eternal joy.

(We praise you that we have been here,
with bread and wine,
to celebrate the coming, the shining, the living, the breaking,
the dying, and the Resurrection
of the Prince of Peace.)

Be praised and glorified, eternal God:
here tonight, this morning, this Christmas Day, and every
    day of the year.

Alan Gaunt

Christmas Blessings

Blessings and Benedictions

May this Christmas be for each of us a time of moving
beyond reason to wonder,
beyond grasping to letting go
and beyond competition to cooperation
in the power of the Babe of Bethlehem.

May the God of the child delight our adult
may the God of the poor confront our wealth,
may the God of the weak mellow our strength,
and the blessing of God in human flesh be perceived
in us and in all people, now and for ever.

May the imagination of the shepherds,
the persistence of the wise men,
the transforming acceptance of Joseph,
the compassion of Mary for her child
and for all the oppressed be in our minds
and actions today and always.

W. L. Wallace
Aotearoa New Zealand

Shining Lights

May our lives and our prayers
be like lights shining
in dark places.
And may the
Blessing of God –
Father,

Son
and Holy Spirit –
fill our hearts and homes
with light this Christmas
and in the new year to come.
Christian Aid

Your Word Made Flesh

Mark 3:21

Bless you, Wise and Holy One,
for your Word made flesh –
For making holy and human
      more intimate
Bless you
for embodying your Word
      not as the founder of
      the-One-True-Religion
      but as a foundling in
  a garden variety family
  – its unwed mother-to-be
      its disputed paternity –
      a family that will wince
      at the public outcry
      over his table-turning words
      will try to take him out
      of the public eye
      to spare the family
      further embarrassment

Bless you, Wise and Holy One,
for not keeping your distance
for making holy
      our garden variety
Norm S. D. Esdon
Canada

New Year

A Litany for New Year's Eve

Candles will need to be lit during the worship

Lighting of the first candle

Leader: We light this candle remembering the children who were baptised this year and whom we have baptised. It beams that all children may be able to grow up receiving affection and protection.

Thus says God: Fear not for I have redeemed you,
I have called you by your name, you are mine.
(Isaiah 43:1)

Silence

Lighting of the second candle

Leader: We light this candle bearing in mind all those married couples who have celebrated wedding anniversaries this year; those who are newly wed, and those who have celebrated silver and golden jubilees.

This light beams for their mutual happiness,
for their courage to break customs,
for their strength to uphold each other even in
   difficult situations;
equipping them with the confidence:

God is love and he who abides in love abides in God and God abides in him. *(I John 4:16)*

Silence

Lighting of the third candle

Leader: We light this third candle remembering all those
who have passed away this year,
all for whom we have mourned and we continue
to mourn.
It illuminates their final way to the eternal home.

If we live we live for the Lord.
If we die we die for the Lord.
But, whether we live or die, we belong to the Lord.
(Romans 14:8)

Silence

Lighting of the fourth candle

Leader: We light this light commemorating all the people,
near or far,
who had to live under wars and have suffered
violence and anxiety.
What they have suffered and endured, needs your
nearness, your comfort and your hope:

And lo, I am with you always, to the close of the
age. *(Matthew 28:20)*

Silence

Lighting of the fifth candle

Leader: We light this candle recollecting all the marvellous
things
we have experienced in the past year.
For greater and smaller moments.

215

This light beams, in order that we continue to
   enjoy the fortunes,
the happiness and everything else that we have
   received as a gift
from the one who comforts us saying:

Rejoice in the Lord always; again I will say,
   Rejoice. *(Philippians 4:4)*

Silence

Lighting of the sixth candle

Leader: We light this candle mindful of the people who have
committed themselves, very much, even put their
lives at risk, for the sake of maintaining freedom and
reconciliation and for facilitating living and working
together without giving way to violence and hatred.
   It burns for those who have not lost hope even in
the midst of experiences of powerlessness and suffering. *(here names may be mentioned)*
   These and many other people have put their hope
in God, who has promised us:

For I certainly know the plans I have for you,
plans for welfare and not for evil and I give you a
future and a hope. *(Jeremiah 29:11)*

Silence

Lighting of the seventh candle

Leader: We light this seventh candle having each and every
one of us in mind, bearing each other in our
strengths and weaknesses, anxieties and hopes.
   It illuminated the ways we have gladly gone
through, and even guided us on paths where we
didn't want to go.

216

It will continue to shine for each and every one of us in the coming year so that we would be able to say:

Commend your ways to the Lord and hope in him, he will make them good. *(Psalm 37:5)*

Silence

Extempore prayers relevant to local communities may be added.

Sinfonia Oecumenica
Germany

Winter Solstice

Small birds,
blowing like ash on the wind,
prepare to leave,
as nights draw in
and days are short.

Small children,
bouncing like corks on water,
prepare for our parties,
as tempers fray
and tasks mount up.

But the darkest and the coldest time
is also the brightest time:
O Christmas Christ,
the radiance around the moon
is not as fair
as the radiance
around your head.

217

O holy one
the majesty of the winter sea
is not as glorious
as your majesty.

At the departing times,
the coldest times
of our lives;
and the times of expectancy,
at the times of intersection,
when hard choices
have to be made
be with us
Prince of Peace.

Grant us warmth
grant us calm
grant us hope
on our journey
into a New Year.

Kate McIlhagga

Part Three:
Epiphany

When hope invites us to journey . . .

Following the Star

Star of Bethlehem

The sky is deep velvet black
yet myriad points of scattered light,
and one sparkles brighter than all,
the resplendent star of Bethlehem.

This is the light that guided
three travellers from the east,
journeying towards the Great Sea,
until the star stopped, hovering above the village.

What is it that would guide
three men of wisdom on a spiritual quest?
What but the hand of God,
drawing them by his created star.

The star was simply the sign
of a brighter burning light.
The birth of a child was the beginning
of light for a darkened world.

Shine on, then, star of Bethlehem
for we too live in deep darkness;
lead us, spiritual thirsting seekers,
to find the light in Jesus, prince of peace.

John Johansen-Berg

The Parable of a Christmas Banquet

Based on Luke 14:15–24

God was preparing the world for a great celebration and sent the Spirit to far away nations, east and west, north and south, telling wise people to 'come for everything is now ready'. And to show them the way the Spirit appeared in the sky, like a star, the brightest of all the stars in heaven.

But many of the wise people began to make excuses, saying: 'I have just obtained some land from a neighbouring country and I must make sure they don't come to take it back.'

Others said: 'I have just bought five new tanks for my army to make it more powerful and we are about to try them out, so please excuse me.'

Another excuse was: 'I have just committed myself to an agreement with a new business partner and I must make sure she understands who is the boss.'

So the Spirit of God continued hovering over the chaos of the world, singing the good news of a wonderful banquet to which everyone was invited. She swept through the streets and alleys of the towns; the fields and valleys of the country, inviting the rich and the poor, the blind and the lame, servants and masters, to follow the light that would lead them to where God was celebrating.

Of all the wise people in the world only three from the East completed the journey, following a star to a banquet in the West. They came seeking peace with gifts from their wealth and hope in their hearts and were led to a stable where the banquet was held.

They met some farm labourers who had left their land when the Spirit told them to go to the town and share the celebration but not many wise people accepted the invitation for they had to fight with their neighbours, strengthen their armies and be master of all and servant to none. There was no time to celebrate with God.

So God sent the Spirit back to the city streets and country

lanes to invite all who were poor to come and celebrate the good news but warned that the wealthy and powerful who had declined to come would not taste the fruits of the Kingdom, found in the stable.

Richard Becher

An Epiphany Prayer (1)

Radiant God, light for all people and all places,
by the guidance of a star you led the Magi
    to worship the Christ Child.
By the light of faith
lead us to worship you in peace and love,
    and guide us in your way.
We pray in the name of Christ,
    light of the world.

Joan McMurtry
Canada

God of Life

God of Life,
Like a promised land,
You invite us to leave our frantic ways.

Like a banquet-laden table
You bid us to restore our empty spirits.

Like a pool of still waters,
You call us to cease our crowded living.

Like a bright and shining star,
You lead us,
And restore our lives of wonder.

Keri Wehlander
Canada

223

Rise Within Us Like a Star

Beckoning God –
  who called the rich to travel toward poverty,
  the wise to embrace your folly,
  the powerful to know their own frailty;
who gave to strangers
  a sense of homecoming in an alien land
and to stargazers
  true light and vision as they bowed to earth –
we lay ourselves open to your signs for us.

Stir us up with holy discontent over a world
which gives its gifts to those
  who have plenty already
  whose talents are obvious
  whose power is recognised;
and help us
both to share our resources with those who have little
and to receive with humility the gifts they bring to us.

Rise within us, like a star,
and make us restless
till we journey forth
to seek our rest in you.

Kate Compston

The Magi

Melchior
How should it be
That one so cast for comfort, as I am,
Should yet embark –
Pale captain of this lurching, desert ship –
On such a voyage?

Who would have guessed that I –
Made martyr to the flaming rage of sun,
All choked by sand,
Still yearning for the fountains of my home –
Should reach the end at last?
Have we not trailed,
From Persia's plateau and its mountain verge,
Across the Plain of Shinar's level green
To Babylon? . . .
And so, the Two Great Rivers crossed,
Straight ploughed the Syrian wastes, for countless weeks,
To set our eyes on Bethlehem?
This have I done with you,
In constant dread of some outlandish death,
With road my sovereign and my lord fatigue,
And only hope and fainting faith to guide.
One thing is sure:
Our journey in itself must mean
That we are held
By that same hand which spins the firmament,
And jettisons new stars.

Paul Hampton

Epiphanic Arrival of the Camel-Drivers

Night is purple. Weird shapes invade a distance
pricked with stars, violent. Imagined, a bird's shriek
splits this desert. A horizon, thin, left white, left nude

vivid with falling dusk a sandstorm pulses,
threatening showers of warm, liquid darkness,
– thick, this dust-month. Rasp: the taste of grit.

Ah, so great these distances! There, by the new mounds,
the wind makes corners: the three young drivers
emerge from blackness. With them, their frozen animals,

crushed to harshness, escape the fierce night sky
close in darkness, stretched. Beneath a slashed star
they carry the tokens: red, blue and silver distinctive,

such richness! And by this, they should be content,
content in this edifice, accepting the sharp sand,
their burden, their heritage, not to question why.

Silhouettes and purple. Crumpled bright foils,
virgin and still as one night in mere thousands.
Three crayons. A child's hand. A projected eye.

Anne Richards

A Journeying Magi's Mood-Swings

My feet are sore.
   The star is dim.
The journey long.
   What a mood I'm in.

I wish I was back
   from where I began.
I'm sick to death
   of this Caravan.

Our route seems wrong.
   The camels are lame.
They've got the hump:
   it's Caspar I blame.

A town ahead!
   Can it really be
the Saviour's home –
   and our destiny?

The star has stopped!
   It's overhead
a stable bare –
   and a manger bed.

Our journey's end!
   At <u>last</u> we see
the Saviour-Child –
   it is <u>truly He.</u>

The Baby smiles.
   The angels sing.
Our gifts, ourselves,
   to you we bring.

Gold is yellow,
   the colour of sun.
I dedicate my wealth
   to the Chosen One.

Now Frankincense,
   to perfume the air.
This most holy smoke
   carries up our prayer.

Myrrh for sorrow,
   which is overcome
when from death to life
   goes the Risen One.

But that's not yet.
   Enough for now
that our Saviour's born –
   king to King I bow.

Oh, Baby Jesus!
　　God's most Beloved Son!
Redeemer of all –
　　<u>You</u> are <u>my</u> chosen One.

Susan Hardwick

The Star

O God, may the star we follow be the steady radiance of
your mystery which we discern only in part but can
for ever trust.

W. L. Wallace
Aotearoa New Zealand

Offering Our Gifts

Epiphany

Epiphany is a jewel
multi-faceted,
flashing colour and light.
Epiphany embraces
the nations of the world,
kneeling on a bare floor
before a child.
Epiphany shows
a man
kneeling in the waters of baptism.
Epiphany reveals
the best is kept for last
as water becomes wine
at the wedding feast.

O Holy One
to whom was given
the gifts of power and prayer,
the gift of suffering,
help us to use
these same gifts
in your way
and in your name.

Kate McIlhagga

On Offering: a Reflection for Christmas

First Voice

> It was the very finest piece of gold
> pure, costly – all I had. Dug from deep earth
> in sweat and darkness, it would buy
> my safety and ensure
> all I would need in age, to ease me into death.
> All through the burning days
> and bitter nights of journeying
> I kept it safe and felt the hard
> smooth weight as my security.
> I had, you understand, earned it
> by just commerce. It was mine.

Second Voice

> The frankincense was rich and rare
> fit for the god of gods
> to breathe my soul's longing
> into his very heart.
> The nightly wonder of the changing sky
> called out from me some strong desire
> to sound infinity, discern
> a light to follow and a path to seek
> to lead me to its core,
> a deity fit for my soul's obeisance.

Third Voice

> Myrrh I had brought.
> I knew the risk of such an enterprise,
> so many starless nights
> wandering in doubt and terror
> along untrodden ways . . .
> There would be death.

It seemed inevitable,
so I was ready, oil and spice prepared
for what would surely come.
I travelled without hope.

*

We left them all upon a stable floor
they seemed at once to find true value laid before
that newborn child.
There in his utter need he seemed
more precious than the finest gold,
fit object of our adoration
hope for our mortal frailty.

It was so. All we had worked and travelled for
our faith and our despair
found their true end in his beginning. So it is.
Amen. So it shall be.

Heather Pencavel

Jubilee

Gift-laden three –
star-followers – reach Bethlehem,
the house of Bread.

They bend the knee
before a displaced Child, for whom
no feast is spread.

Self-centred, we –
star-struck by the Millennium
(or bored instead?) –

seem not to see
how we are poor unless we come
and share our bread . . .

Make Jubilee! –
and break the exploiters' chains. The time
is ripe to tread

new paths: walk free!
In each heart build a Bethlehem
where all are fed.

Kate Compston

A Eucharist Prayer

Father of all blessings, we give you thanks and praise
for Jesus the Light of the world, the light that
no darkness can overpower;
we thank you that you have called us from darkness
to walk in the light;
we thank you for the insight of the wise men,
who by their gifts showed us
that all life is a gift;
with them, the angels and archangels
and all who live in the light,
we praise you, singing,

Holy, holy, holy is the Lord . . .

Accept our praises now, Lord God,
as we remember Jesus,
who, on the night before he died,
took bread and wine, gave you thanks
and offered them to his friends, saying,
this is my body, this is my blood.
Eat and drink to remember me.

Come freshly to us now, Lord God,
and as we offer you our lives,
renew in us your gifts:
the gold of our potential,
the incense of our prayers and aspirations,
the myrrh of healing for our pain;
feed us and nourish us,
that we may grow in the life of Christ;
fill us with your Spirit
that we may overflow with your love,
and transform the world with your glory.
Glory, glory, glory to the Lord . . .

Ann Lewin

An Epiphany Blessing

These words, which come from the Dead Sea Scrolls, may be offered both as a blessing upon our Christmas celebrations and a prayer for the needs of the land of Jesus' birth.

May the Lord bless you with all good and keep you from
   all evil;
may he give light to your heart with loving wisdom,
and be gracious to you with eternal knowledge;
may he lift up his loving countenance upon you for
   eternal peace.
Amen

Christian Aid

The Baptism of Christ

The Baptism of Christ

Thoughts for reflection

The descent into the waters of our spirit is a journey into the presence of divinity.

Through immersion in waters of life there comes the realisation that to be a child of earth is to be a child of God.

The primary water of baptism is the life-giving water of our Inner Christ, source of limitless sustenance for our journey.

There is no immersion into the heart of God without immersion into the life of the world; for the life of the world is contained within the heart of God.

All human beings are children of God but not all live in the awareness that there is 'that of God' within them.

Prayer

O God of the waters, as Jesus Christ descended into the waters of Jordan, help us to become immersed in the waters of nature and the waters of the spirit that as your children we may see you in all things.

W. L. Wallace
Aotearoa New Zealand

Our Common Baptism

Creator Spirit,
who in the beginning hovered over the waters,
and at Jesus' baptism descended in the form
of a dove;
who at Pentecost was poured out under the
signs of fire and wind –
come to us;
open our hearts and minds
for the life-giving word
in the covenant of baptism,
so that we may listen
and be renewed by your power.

Sinfonia Oecumenica
Germany

God in Unexpected Places

An Epiphany Prayer (2)

O God, our light, our beauty, our rest:
With the appearance of your Son
>you have brought us into your new creation.

Form us into your people and order our lives in you;
>through Christ, the living One

Amen.

Gail Ramshaw
Canada

God at Epiphany

The God who at Epiphany is revealed in our midst is a human being whose presence is honest, exemplary and transforming. Honest, because in the scope of a single human life he climbs the heavens with us and goes into the depths of hell with us, such is his sensitivity, intuition and pastoral care.

Exemplary, because in the way he responded to others and their needs, we are shown how to live with the same clarity and generosity. Transforming, because in embracing his Passion, humanity and its potential were changed for ever.

This Epiphany season, as the Western world ask what manner of future we are speeding towards, how can we influence its shape, and encourage the growth of justice and peace, I pray that the Body of Christ will see how we are already living in Christ's honest, exemplary and transformative way. Despite our frailty and our many failings, the renewed life is being offered to the world. Your loving is part of that. Thanks be to God.

O God who comes to us –
in the time of dearth,
        and in the time of feasting,
in the time of anxiety,
        and in the time of opportunity,
in the hour of loss,
        and in the hour of given wealth,
in the hour of breaking,
        and in the hour when a new foundation is being laid,
in the day of chaos,
        and in the day of renewal,
in the day of powerlessness,
        and in the day when we witness
        to a grace that is not our own –

O God who comes to us,
love in us
and in the midst of our community.

Stand revealed
as light and hope and truth,
that whatever the future brings,
your peace may grow,
your joy inspire,
your trust in us and in the world
be justified
at last.

Julie M. Hulme

Recognise and Respond

John 1:10–18

Creator God
with the dawning of each new day
you reveal yourself again to us.

Show us how to recognise you
       in the warmth of the sun and refreshing rain
       in uncurling buds and falling leaves
       in the arrival and departure of the swallows.
Forgive us for the times when we fail to recognise you.

Open our eyes, help us to see.

Saviour Christ
you broke into time revealing God to us,
you gave us the new law of love.
Teach us how to recognise you
       in our neighbours – rich or poor,
       at work, unemployed, the victims of war,
       the new-born and the dependent parent.
Forgive us for the times when we fail to recognise you.

Open our hearts, help us to love.

Holy Spirit
you are sent to empower us,
you are within us waiting to work.
Enable us to respond to you
       when another charity envelope lands on our mat
       when a neighbour wants to talk
       when we need to uphold our faith.
Forgive us for the times when we fail to respond to you.

Open our lives, help us to serve.

Heather Johnston

God, in Whom is Peace

God, in whom is peace,
we praise you.

We praise the unexpected gift of peace
which steals softly into our frenzied activity
and gives us still spaces of tranquillity.

We praise the hard-earned work of peace
which struggles through our anger and bitterness
to nudge us into forgiveness and new beginnings.

We praise the shining dream of peace
which beckons and inspires us
to confront violence and injustice
with words of hope and acts of commitment.

We praise the mysterious peace
which lies beyond our imagination
our efforts and our dreams –
your gift of peace to a longing world.

Jan Berry

Travelling On

Travelling On

When hope invites us to journey
elusive, beckoning onward
but never in our grasp:
God of wisdom and promise
give us courage to travel on.

When dreams glimmer in the distance,
fading, clouded and hidden
or shining with new brightness:
God of wisdom and promise
give us courage to travel on.

When established patterns collapse
into the uncertainty of the unknown
and security dissolves into a memory:
God of wisdom and promise
give us courage to travel on.

When the illusion of success
threatens to divert us
and silence our souls' yearning:
God of wisdom and promise
give us courage to travel on.

When we think our journey has ended
in the star-lit glow
only to find the end is a new beginning:
God of wisdom and promise
give us courage to travel on.

Jan Berry

240

Epiphany Hymn

Written for Lis Mullen and the Women in Ministry Network

Deep in the darkness a starlight is gleaming,
Calling us out from the safety of home.
God of the questions, the mystery of dreaming,
Lighten our journey into the unknown.

Out of the darkness the voices are crying,
Terror and fear screaming loud in the night.
God of the hurting, of innocence dying,
Fire us with anger to struggle for right.

Still in the darkness we search for your healing,
Hoping for meaning to comfort our fear.
God of the silence, of unspoken feeling,
Teach us the wisdom to make your truth clear.

On through the darkness we follow your leading,
Searching for joy and a refuge to stay.
God of our longing, the bliss we are seeking,
Journey with us to the brightness of day.

Tune: Epiphany Hymn

Jan Berry

Setting Out on the Pilgrim Way

*The Church of Norway supports a renewal of the pilgrim movement
in which a new religious longing of the people finds its expression by
special religious materials, pilgrim services and the creation of a
pilgrim ministry.*

We are now at the beginning of our pilgrimage, the time for
departure has come.

241

To be a pilgrim is to be on one's way – on one's way towards a goal.

The word 'pilgrim' is derived from the Latin word 'peregrinus' i.e. strange, foreign. The medieval pilgrims came from far away and were looked upon as strangers where they came.

A pilgrimage, however, is not an escape from life itself, to alienate us from it.

Rather, it is a pilgrimage with God in order to be in life.

The pilgrimage is an old tradition which reminds us that life is a waking from birth to death with God – of, by and to Him.

Life is a process with God, with ourselves and with other people. It is a movement from exodus to the goal, with new perceptions along the way, accompanied by changes of course and new movements.

A pilgrimage is, as such, an outer wandering as well as an inner voyage, a part of a life journey.

When we now, in the hands of God, venture ourselves into new territory, let us remind each other of God's promises on the journey of life.

A Prayer

Lord God, Heavenly Father,
we thank you for protecting those who seek you
and for your guiding of those who hope for you.
We pray for your blessing and that you bless us
now when we enter our pilgrimage.
Save us from all evil, let no harm come upon us.
Protect our body and our soul.
Help us to wander with an open mind for what you will
    reveal to us on our way,
and when we reach our goal, help us to listen to your voice
and be open to your renewal of our faith and our life.

Lord, bless us and keep us.
Lord, let your face shine upon us,
and give us your peace.
Amen

Sinfonia Oecumenica
Germany

Pilgrimage

From   dependency to empowerment
individualism to community
puritanism to celebration
captivity to liberation
static to dynamic
compartments to the whole
square to circle
straight line to curve
mechanical to organic
known to mystery.

W. L. Wallace
Aotearoa New Zealand

Magi's Pilgrimage: Found

Footsore, yes. But now at the end of this endless trail
with autumn come
and changes the order of the day, the holy grail
draws us home.

It is unexpected, the finding of it (I'd rather say
the being found):
we'd looked in tip-toe places, traced the star's white way –
but missed the ground

from which we grow, in whom we live, and where the leaves
turn to gold . . .
Perhaps we, too, may cast sham loves for one who weaves
new from old . . .

And we are reached for, energized. This autumn Son
heralds our spring.
We thought we'd finished, find we've only now begun
our journeying . . .

Kate Compston

Setting Out

Peace to this house
>　where you can put your feet up and relax;
>　where the welcome goes beyond
>　acceptance of the like-minded;
>　where doing your duty to the poor
>　　　is more than a 'nice little earner' for the kingdom.

Peace to this land
>　where the less privileged
>　are empowered to be equal partners with the rest;
>　where judgement is meted fairly
>　without an underlying agenda
>　of revenge or retribution;
>　where the desire to heal
>　is in the spirit of the people.

Peace to this world
>　where we progressively respect other forms of life;
>　where conflict is addressed creatively;
>　where burdens are shared, and the harvest is for everyone,
>　for the worker deserves her pay.

O God, make us pilgrims
with judgement in mind
and salvation as our aim
always on the move towards you.

Janet Wootton

Wise Words for the Epiphany Season

There are arguments to be had about the underlying values and quality of contemporary culture but no-one, surely, can fail to recognise that it is immensely varied and complicated. Beside the hopelessness and despair there is moral serious-ness, a desire to find the good life in a confusing and brutal world. It is in many ways a more thoughtful, kinder culture, more concerned about injustice and discrimination than any before it. Traditional theology and philosophy may have run out of steam but people are discovering the sacred in new and unexpected spaces, in work for social justice, in new kinds of commitment and public ritual. Alongside the dreary repetition, the dross and kitsch of contemporary culture, there is plenty of surprise and invention. Fusions and cross-fertilisations of different ethnic traditions and especially the impact of new communications technologies have stirred up the cultural gene pool. It is interesting out there. Intelligent listening, sifting and discernment would be welcome.

Brendan Walsh

Soft the Evening Shadows Fall

Soft the evening shadows fall,
    still journey on;
darkness soon be over all,
    still journey on.
Weary now, and travel-worn,
night must come before the morn:
where will Mary's Son be born?
    still journey on.

Shepherds, hasten from the fold;
    this God has done.
Here in human form behold
    this God has done.

245

Christ the Lord of David's line,
born a Saviour and a sign,
King immortal, child divine,
    this God has done.

Kings who from the east afar
    still journey on,
seeking Christ beneath a star,
    still journey on.
For his worship incense bring,
gold to crown an infant King,
myrrh to mark his suffering,
    still journey on.

Lord of all, enthroned above,
    God sent his Son.
Gift of everlasting love,
    God sent his Son.
He himself a ransom gave,
bowed himself to cross and grave,
came himself to seek and save,
    God sent his Son.

So the Christmas story tell;
    still journey on.
At the last shall all be well;
    still journey on.
Love be ours, and joy and praise,
one with Christ to walk his ways,
in his service all our days
    still journey on.

7.4.7.4.7.7.7.4 metre

Timothy Dudley-Smith

Flights to Strange Lands

Flight into Egypt

Matthew 2:13–15

While shepherds and Magi adored the Child, Joseph had been in the background, quietly watching and caring for his wife: now he was urgently called to action to protect the Son of God. Escaping the jealous rage of Herod, they fled southward to Egypt, the land from which their ancestors had been brought out of slavery.

Prayer:

We give thanks for all who protect the weak and vulnerable and pray that they may be given strength to fulfil their calling; and for the divine love that uses our frailty to support one another in need. We pray for guidance in all times of danger and uncertainty.

We do not open ourselves fully to God's ways of guiding; we stand aside while others act to help those in need. Make us more ready to care not only for those near to us but for the stranger and the outcast, the homeless and those who flee from persecution.

V	God sent his Son into the world
R	**To bring us to eternal life.**
V	Let us bless the Lord
R	**Thanks be to God.**

God's protecting darkness concealed their flight
from the dark jealousy that feared the defenceless.

247

They had to leave the Promised Land,
go back through the wilderness to the place of slavery.

God who had carried his people in the wandering years
made the return journey in a mother's arms,
divine power diminished into a bundle of humanity.
They were not the first to flee from tyranny
or the last to stumble across a strange frontier,
to seek safety among alien faces
when the familiar took on a face of doom.

In time the Child would welcome the stranger,
the outcast,
the despised,
the unprotected,
with a royal love that kings dared not feel
because the ground beneath the throne might be shaken.

Prayer:

On wanderers without a home:
Lord have mercy.

On refugees driven by war and violence:
Lord have mercy.

On my hardness of heart when help is needed:
Lord have mercy.

Raymond Chapman

A Litany for Refugees and Asylum Seekers

Leader: Lord Jesus, your parents were forced to flee from
Herod's murderous fear. Have pity on those who
flee their homes today.

Lord, hear our prayer for them.

All: **And let our cry come unto you.**

Leader: Lord Jesus, you travelled a dangerous road to Egypt. Have mercy on those who travel on unsafe boats, in the back of lorries, or with help of traffickers because they can find no other way.

Lord, hear our prayer for their safety.

All: **And let our cry come unto you.**

Leader: Lord Jesus, you were born in a stable because there was no room for your parents in the inn. You came to your own, and your own received you not. So you understand the anxiety of those who arrive in our country as aliens and find themselves unwanted and vilified.

Lord, hear our prayer for aliens and strangers in our country.

All: **And let our cry come unto you.**

Leader: Lord Jesus, you saved your moral condemnation for the self-righteous and the oppressor. Save us from condemning those who come here in economic desperation looking for a better life for themselves and for their children.

Lord, hear our prayer for all whose aspirations are thwarted.

All: **And let our cry come unto you.**

Leader: Lord Jesus, we feel helpless about the collapsed economies of Eastern Europe, of Africa, when we hear about countries torn apart by conflict, or populations whose hopes rot away under corrupt regimes whilst we prosper. Help us to find ways to promote the common good of humankind.

Lord, hear our prayer for a just and peaceable world.

All: **And let our cry come unto you.**

Leader: Lord Jesus, you were condemned after an unfair trial. We pray that those who apply for asylum may be treated humanely, find the advice they need and be given a fair hearing.

Lord, hear our prayer for justice and humanity to be shown to all.

All: **And let our cry come unto you.**

Leader: Lord Jesus, Egyptian Christians are proud that their ancestors provided a refuge for you. Help us to be glad that we in our turn can offer safety to people who have suffered persecution.

Lord, hear our prayer and give us glad and generous hearts.

All: **And let our cry come unto you.**

Leader: Lord Jesus, you came not to condemn but to save. We bring to you those people who are refused asylum and removed from Britain. Some spent all their savings on getting here, and must now go back to destitution. Help us to resist the temptation to say it serves them right.

Lord, hear our prayer to be saved from vindictiveness.

All: **And let our cry come unto you.**

Leader: Lord Jesus, for using refugees and asylum seekers
as scapegoats, forgive us;
As we try to be more generous and understanding,
renew a right spirit within us;
As we join in the struggle for a better and fairer
world, enable us and give us courage;
And may your kingdom come and your will be
done, on earth as it is in heaven.

Louise Pirouet

Lord, We Pray for Those Living on the Edge of Communities

Lord, we pray for those living on the edge of communities:

For women trapped in violent relationships, afraid to leave
because they have nowhere safe to take their children, living
each day in fear, making the kids keep quiet in case they get
hit:
Help us to love one another as you love us.

For asylum seekers, often running for their lives and risking
everything, yet now facing suspicion, forced to move from
place to place, unable to get work or claim benefits:
Help us to love one another as you love us.

For young people leaving care, alone and unsupported without the safety net of a family, fending for themselves on the
streets:
Help us to love one another as you love us.

For those who sleep on the pavement tonight because all the hostels are full:
   Help us to love one another as you love us.

May we grow in love and faithfulness as we build your new community on earth.

Rachel Lampard and Jennie Richmond

God By Extension

Gathering God,
extending your love
to the far off
and the refugees within:
embracing them
in a dance of delightful renewal,
   Praise be to you.

Giving God,
extending your arms
on a cross,
opened out to the limits,
to gather in unity
heaven and earth,
   Praise be to you.

Guiding God,
extending your presence
through our lives:
that by your Spirit baptising
with grace and truth,
your will becomes flesh,
   Praise be to you.

Stephen Brown

Joseph's Story

The immediacy of the holy family's departure into exile is striking. The need for immediate flight from danger is a typical situation for the majority of refugees. As the church in The Gambia, we are confronted daily with the pain of refugees who have fled from conflict.

Let me share with you the story of another Joseph, from Sierra Leone. He was working with his two small children in the family garden several hundred metres away from their home when rebels hit the village. The children hid. Joseph ran to search for his wife and his other children. He found the house on fire, terror and chaos in the village. But no sign of his family. He came straight to The Gambia with the two children but has since returned in search of his wife whom he had heard was alive but injured. As with the biblical Joseph he has placed the lives of himself and his family in God's hands seeing Him as his only hope.

S. Tilewa Johnson
The Gambia

Christmas Cards

Pictures of the Holy Family travelling down to Egypt. Mary riding on a donkey with her baby well-wrapped up in her arms, Joseph walking alongside under a deep blue star-studded sky, a palm tree or two, an angel keeping guard. A holy, romantic scene.

Lord, you arrived safely in Egypt
though we don't know what the journey was really like.
Today's refugees may have to travel dangerously
to reach a place of safety:
in unseaworthy boats on the Mediterranean;
in the backs of lorries across the Channel;
a desperate few fatally in the wheel-house of a jumbo-jet.

Protect them on their journeys:
from the rapacity of those who profit from their helplessness;
from the greed of wealthy nations
who want to keep too much of the world's wealth for
    themselves;
from the unscrupulous who may prey on them when they
    arrive;
and may an angel keep guard over them.

Louise Pirouet

Here Stands a Stranger, Who Is She?

Here stands a stranger, who is she?
We do not know. What do we see,
someone who threatens you and me?
Is she a foe, or friend?

Here stands a person, young or old,
seeking asylum, so we're told.
How does he fit your frame or mould?
Is he your foe or friend?

Here stands a child: assess her need.
What should we offer so we heed
her cry of hunger, so we feed
this child? This foe? This friend?

Here stands a person, this time, you.
The choice is yours. What will you do
to ask this stranger in, or sue
this foe, who could be friend?

Here is a mirror, see your face.
What do you offer; hatred, grace,
now in this very time and place,
to Christ you call your friend.

Tune: 8.8.8.6 metre

Andrew Pratt

Christ from Heaven's Glory Come

Christ from heaven's glory come,
in a stable make your home.
Helpless new-born babe-in-arms,
dream of terror's night-alarms.
Lullaby, my little love,
Herod's troops are on the move.

Cradled on a mother's knee,
immigrant and refugee,
talking, walking hand in hand,
homeless in a foreign land,
Child of Mary, full of grace,
exile of an alien race.

Christ whose hand the hungry fed,
stones were yours in place of bread;
Christ whose love our ransom paid,
by a kiss at last betrayed;
friendless now, and nothing worth,
join the outcasts of the earth.

Soon the soldiers' jest is done,
'They will reverence my Son.'
On the gallows hang him high,
'By our law he ought to die.'

Perished, all the flower of youth:
Wash your hands, for what is truth?

*

Christ who once at Christmas came,
move our hearts who name your Name.
By your body, bring to birth
truth and justice, peace on earth,
sinners pardoned, love restored:
reign among us, risen Lord!

7.7.7.7.7.7 metre

Timothy Dudley-Smith

Prayers for Refugees

All: The word belongs to God
the earth and all its people.

How good and how lovely it is
to live together in unity.

Love and faith come together,
justice and peace join hands.

If the Lord's disciples keep silent
these stones would shout aloud.

Lord, open our lips
and our mouth shall proclaim your praise.

World Council of Churches

Confession:

Leader: Most merciful God,

All: We confess that we are in bondage to sin and cannot free ourselves. We have sinned against you in thought, word and deed by what we have done and what we have left undone. We have not loved you with our whole heart: we have not loved our neighbours as ourselves. For the sake of your son, Jesus Christ, have mercy on us. Help us and give us the grace of the Holy Spirit so that our sinful life may be transformed and we may have eternal life. Through our Lord, Jesus Christ. Amen.

Reading: Matthew 25:31–46

Intercessions

Take a few moments to reflect on this season of Epiphany and how we can be enabled to show compassion to all refugees and asylum seekers.

The leader should intercede on behalf of refugees and asylum seekers making the prayer relevant to your local situation. Also, prayers may be offered by any member of the congregation.

Prayer of Commitment:

Leader: Sisters and brothers, let us stand and affirm what we have discovered of God's will in the company of each other.
That we worship one God,
Father, Son and Holy Spirit,
in whose image we are made,
to whose service we are summoned,
by whose presence we are renewed.

All: **This we believe.**

Leader: That it is central to the mission of Christ
   to participate, by word and action,
   in the struggles of the poor for justice,
   to share justly the earth's land and resources,
   to rejoice in the diversity of human culture,
   to preserve human life in all its beauty and frailty,
   to accompany the uprooted and welcome the
      stranger,
   and to witness – every day – to the love of God for
      all people of the earth.

All: **This we believe.**

Leader: That we are called to become
   The Church of the Stranger,
   to open ourselves
   to the transforming power of the Holy Spirit
   which may come to us through the foreigner,
   to take the risk of speaking out on behalf
   of those who are different from us,
   and to see that when we minister to the stranger,
   the uprooted,
   we are serving our Lord and Saviour.

All: **This we believe.**

Leader: That God has called the church into being
   to be the servant of the kingdom,
   to be a sign of God's new order,
   to celebrate in the streets and fields
   of every land the liturgy of heaven.

All: **This we believe.**

Leader: That Christ,
   fully aware of our differences,
   prays that we might be one
   so that the world may believe.

All: This we believe,
and to this we are committed
for the love of God
in the way of Christ,
by the power of the Holy Spirit.
Amen

Blessing:

All: We go now as sojourners in the land,
pilgrims passing through.
We go to accept responsibility for the land
we are passing through.
The kingdom of God is neither here
nor there.
The kingdom is among us.
Amen

World Council of Churches
Liturgy written by the Jesuit Refugee Service

Living, Loving God

Living, loving God,
we are told that Mary, Joseph and Jesus travelled
as refugees
to Egypt.
They were strangers
in a strange land
separated from
loved ones,
their community and
familiar surroundings.

We are told that during his ministry
Jesus surrounded himself with
strangers,

259

marginalised people and
the outcasts of society.

We remember now
women . . .
men . . .
children . . .
who are separated from their families,
homes
communities
because of
selfishness
broken relationships
greed
hatred
famine
war.

Encourage us,
enable us
to move
out of our comfort,
our complacency and
get alongside the sad,
the strangers
who cry out
for understanding
for help
for love.

Motivate us through compassion
to be the prime movers
to bring about
a change in attitudes
in our communities and
to open our homes,
to give shelter

and sanctuary
and no-strings-attached love
to people . . . who
need us to be
Christ-like.

Geoff Duncan

The Presentation

Mary and Joseph Came to the Temple

Mary and Joseph
Came to the temple,
Brought the boy Jesus,
Offered him there.
People were waiting
Wanting to greet him,
Long had they sought him,
Solace for care.

Anna had prayed there,
Widowed, long waiting;
Worshipping God by
Day and by night.
Now she is praising,
Filled with elation;
Here is God's promise,
Christ is her light.

Simeon sings now
God proffers blessing,
Brilliantly gilding
Dawn of this day;
Light in the darkness,
Never extinguished,
Light of all nations,
Light up our way.

Tune: Bunessan, Temple Song, or Mary and Joseph

Andrew Pratt

Simeon

The old man spoke,
his eyes full of wonder.
He said:
for all these long Decembers,
all those Advents,
I waited and hoped and longed
for the Christ-child.
But it was only
this Christmas night,
as I knelt by the Crib,
I realised, after all these years,
His greater, deeper, truer longing
for me.

Anthea Dove

Through Darkness the Light Still Shines

*I have seen with my own eyes the deliverance you
have made (Luke 2:30)*

*This child is destined to be a sign that will be rejected;
and you too will be pierced to the heart (Luke 2:34–5)*

So through the generations,
in the familiar words of the Nunc Dimittis,
men and women have echoed Simeon's Song
of thankfulness and praise.
In his arms he held the child
destined to be the Saviour of the world,
yet it was a bittersweet vision
which had been granted to Simeon.
He saw that joy would be mixed with sorrow,
that this child would grow to face rejection and suffering
before, through his sacrifice,
our deliverance could be effected.

Lord, we thank you
that though Christmas is over
the Christmas message of a Saviour remains.
We thank you
that though all the presents
have been opened
the greatest gift of all
can still bring us joyous surprises.
We may for a time have eaten well,
if not always wisely;
but through your sacrificial giving of yourself
you offer us the bread and water of life
that we may be sustained all our days
and by your mercy brought at last
to your eternal kingdom.

Edmund Banyard

Praise to You, Son of the Most High, Who Has Put On Our Body

A Reading from a hymn of Ephrem of Syria

Praise to you, Son of the Most High, who has put on our
   body!

Into the holy temple Simeon carried the Christ-child
and sang a lullaby to him:
>   'You have come, Compassionate One,
>   having pity on my old age, making my bones enter
>   into Sheol in peace. By you I will be raised
>   out of the grave into paradise.'

Anna embraced the child: she placed her mouth
upon his lips, and then the spirit rested
upon her lips, like Isaiah
whose mouth was silent until a coal drew near
to his lips and opened his mouth.

Anna was aglow with the spirit of his mouth.
She sang him a lullaby:
> 'Royal Son,
> despised son, being silent, you hear;
> hidden, you see; concealed, you know;
> God-man, glory to your name.'

Even the barren heard and came running with their
provisions.
The Magi are coming with their treasures.
The barren are coming with their provisions.
Provisions and treasures were heaped up suddenly among
the poor.

The barren woman Elizabeth cried out as she was
accustomed,
> 'Who has granted to me, blessed woman,
> to see your Babe by whom heaven and earth are filled?
> Blessed is your fruit
> that brought forth the cluster on a barren vine.'

Praise to you, Son of the Most High, who has put on our
body!

Ephrem of Syria

The Presentation in the Temple

*What does the Lord God ask of you except to act justly, to love
tenderly and to walk humbly with your God? (Micah 6:8)*

In the people we meet on the Feast of the Presentation these
qualities are in evidence throughout: justice, tenderness,
humility, as the child Jesus comes to his Father's house for the
first time.

Simeon, Anna, Mary and Joseph welcome and cherish him.
Mary and Joseph bring with them the offering of the poor as

265

they make their way among the great colonnades of the Court of the Gentiles towards the Court of the Women. The aged Simeon recognises the promised Messiah and takes the child in his arms. Simeon is an icon of the Heavenly Father who accepts this offering of his Son, an offering which will be consummated on the Cross. In his infancy he is placed in Simeon's arms: at the end of his life Jesus commended himself into the hands of his heavenly Father as he breathes his last.

Mary hears that Jesus is to be a Light to the Gentiles, the Glory of Israel but also a dividing sword, a Child destined to cause his Mother much anguish.

A candle is given to us at Baptism as a sign that Christ is to be our light and companion through life. Every day, every minute, Mary is placing Jesus in our arms so that we may recognise and cherish him. Yet so often our attention is elsewhere and we miss his presence. We are like the crowds in the temple during Jesus' presentation. Like them we see just an anonymous infant, one among many, and we take no further notice. We do not recognise God in human guise.

Among all the worshippers only Simeon and Anna had a glimpse into the real nature of the Child in Mary's arms and they welcomed him with love. The Spirit revealed to them who the child really was. They could not have obtained or merited this knowledge by themselves.

However, Simeon and Anna had done what they could. Like Mary and Joseph they had acted justly, loved tenderly, walked humbly with God and so the Spirit was able to take them further. They recognised the Lord and could depart in peace, rejoicing.

The Presentation is a beautiful lyrical feast; a feast of the temple, of Mary as light-bearer, of Jesus as Lord. We have to enter into the reality, take the child Jesus into our own arms, open our hearts, like Mary, ready for the Word of the Lord to pierce us, showing us our weaknesses and sinfulness, our need of a Saviour. Only when we recognise this need and try to be faithful can the Spirit reveal all he wants to give us.

A Child lies sleeping in darkest night,
Radiant and soft in the candlelight.

He is the one who is Israel's glory,
The Gentile's God in the Temple story.

Joyfully let us acclaim him, beholding
The Mother, the Son of the Father enfolding.

But the silent Word once in Temple shown
Is only by silent beholding now known.

And the heart must be pierced by pain and by joy
From the light that flows out from this innocent Boy.

If I hold him close he will break and burn,
But only that I too may glow in my turn.

Elizabeth Obbard

Shine On

Christ the Door

The door to every heart lies within.
The door to the earth lies within.
The door to the mystery lies within.
The door to everywhere lies within.
For the way of God lies within.

W. L. Wallace
Aotearoa New Zealand

Let Every Word

Let every word
be the fruit
of action and reflection.
Reflection alone
without action
or tending towards it
is mere theory,
adding its weight when we are overloaded
with it already
and it has led to despair.
Action alone
without reflection
is being busy
pointlessly.
Honour the Word eternal
and speak
to make
a new world possible.

Dom Helder Camara
Brazil

Invocation to the Christ of the Four Directions

We call upon the Christ of the East:

You, whose birth was foretold by prophets,
You, whose birth was heralded by the eastern star,
You, whose birth was surrounded by the radiance of angels,
You, whose birth was illuminated by the heavenly hosts,
You, whose birth was attended by watchful shepherds,
You, whose birth was visited by wise ones from the East,
You, whose birth bespoke the dawning of a new age of love
    and peace,

As the sunrise signals a new day,
O Christ of the East:
Bring now new vision and imagination into our minds.
Purify us with Your fire of clarity and burn in our hearts.
Humble us, with Bethlehem's birth, in knowledge and love
    of you.
Throw out, in us, new shoots and branches, as the stem of
Jesse's rod did bloom again through your incarnation.
Soar us to the heights of angel/eagle vision.
Show us the lion and the lamb lying down together.
Illuminate our bodies with the light of your presence.

O You, whose birth brings a peace which passes
All understanding, raise us to a new awareness.

O Christ of the East, Sun of God,
We call upon you.
Amen.

We call upon the Christ of the South:

You, who in fresh youth were drawn, unsated, to grow in
    wisdom in the temple.

You, who grew in stature as you grew in spiritual strength,
You, who through abiding trust in your Father, taught others
to trust in you,
You, who transformed fish and bread into a midday meal for
thousands,
You, who at a wedding, led many to shed old skins of self as
you shed old wine skins for new wine.
You, who, in parable, planted abundant energy in those who
truly listened.
You, who in healing touch and word, brought wholeness to
the ill and broken.

As the warm south wind caresses the summer,
O Christ of the South;

Enter our hearts and heal us.
Grow us back to laughter, trust and innocence.
Poke us, as with the quills of the porcupine, provoking us to
learn.
Warm our souls with gentleness,
Refresh our wilted wills,
Cultivate in us new green, growing aspects to our lives.
Reconnect us to the web of life.

O You, who are the fruit of the earth, take up residence in us
now and be the One in whom our destiny lies. Nurture us,
fertilise us, flower us in your grace. O Christ of the South,
cultivator of souls,
We call upon you.
Amen.

We call upon the Christ of the West:

You, who saw the harvest bounty of your mission,
You, who reaped the wisdom of the Spirit,
You, who sat in thanksgiving with your friends,
You, who were betrayed at the price of your body and your
blood,

You, who prayed alone in the garden contemplating that
which could not be altered.
You, who understood that transfiguration comes through the
gateway of death,
You, who bore your death as an impeccable warrior for us all.

As sunset and twilight come upon us,
O Christ of the West:

Comfort us with your knowledge of the darkness.
Encourage us, like the black bear, to enter the cave of con-
templation.
Lead us, in silence and solitude, to see that which we must
allow to die in us.
Teach us to pray, 'Thy will be done.'
Cleanse the thoughts of our hearts,
Protect us as we drink from the chalice of decision.
Give us the pure water of righteousness to assuage our thirst
at death.

O You, who shake hands with thunder and are the willing
servant of surrender, walk with us into darkness, there to
befriend the shadows.
Take the raven of death that we may watch and wait and be
transformed.
O Christ of the West, protector of souls, we call upon you.
Amen.

O Christ of the North:

You, who bore the pain of Calvary,
You, who blessed the ones who cursed you,
You, who lay in the tomb, germinating resurrection,
You, who even as you entered Hades, challenged those
around you,
You, who in your rising, fulfilled the expectations and
prophecies of the ancestors.

You, who in your ascending, gave the promise of a new
   covenant to the beings of the future,
You, who in the snowy cold of mid winter, began the quiet
   cycle of birth again,
   in our hearts as we tell your story.

As we enter our own winters of death and seeding,
O Christ of the North:

Keep vigil with us as we bear the harsh, cold times of our
   lives.
Wrap us in cloaks of clarity and strength when the strong,
   north winds of challenge blow around us.
Weave pure and crystalline threaded shrouds of
   understanding around us as we lie in death.
Give us the grace and silence of the snowy owl to go within
   and seek our inner wisdom.
Help us to remember to call upon the many blessings and
   gifts of our elders for our endurance and creativity.
Keep us in honesty and truth with the remembrance of your
   fidelity and faithfulness even unto crucifixion.
Nourish us with deep sleep and perfect rest as we
   cradle the seeds of new life within us.

O You, who were the source and power of Life before the
   elders –
And who will be so after those yet unborn, be with us as we
   cycle through the spiral of life, death and rebirth.
O Christ of the North, Holy Guardian of us all, we call upon
   you.
Amen.

Suzanne Fageol
USA

272

Shine On

Shine on, shine on, star of Bethlehem
Shine as on that night
Shine on, shine on, star of Bethlehem
Teach us how to show your light.

Garth Hewitt

Part Four:
Supplement of New Material

The Candle

The candle
gives light to us,
the flame reflects and flickers,
like a spiralling shape
rising up to illuminate,
directing, upwards,
gentle and calming.
The flickering of a candle
gives a warm and a comfortable feeling,
lighting up a room,
lighting our way.
Christmas candles reflecting a birth
of a King,
reflecting our own Christian birth.

The advent candles are special.
They bring hope, joy, peace and love,
burning brightly,
showing us the way to Christmas Eve,

to a birth of a baby,
Jesus, who was born long ago,
bringing with him and in him
these words:
'I am the light of the world.'

This Christmas time, may
the light from these candles
stay with us, burning brightly
in the days to come,

lighting our way, beginning from
now to the next
Christmas Eve with even more
peace, joy hope and love.

Thank you, flickering candles of advent light
And a faith that may be born anew.

Barbara Oakes

Magnificat for Three Choirs

(Written after hearing the three cathedral choirs gathered in different places in Winchester Cathedral, UK sing Victoria's Magnificat)

Encircled by music,
Harmonies swirling from
Choir to answering choir,
Swelling at last to join in
High thanksgiving . . .
It was like being
Drawn into the Rublev icon.

The three conductors,
Watching each other
With courteous attention,
Drew from each choir
Sounds of great beauty,
Invited us to join
Their creativity, and
Offer our hearts
With their Magnificat.

Ann Lewin

Expectation

My soul magnifies the Lord
    and I dance with God who liberates me,
for she has remembered with love
    the whispered song of her shadow.
Surely, from now on my story will be
    handed down to all generations.
For the One who is Love
    has cradled my life in her arms
    and beautiful is her name.
Her tenderness enfolds our brokenness
    through all generations.

Her voice clamours in shouts of justice,
wrenching free the grip of the abuser.
She gathers the abused to her breast,
    her milk nurturing those who seek her,
    according to the promise given to
        our grandmothers,
    to Sarah and Hagar
        and their children forever.

The United Reformed Church

Heirs to the Kingdom

God of the generations,
    we celebrate with you in the miracle of new life,
    the wonder of the first glimpse into new-born eyes,
    the excitement of the first grasp of tiny fingers,
    as we name the promise of future hope.

From age to age, may we grow in faith

279

God of the generations
>we praise you for the joy and pain of parenting,
>from the thrill of first footsteps, to the worry of
>>leaving home,
>from the tears of teething, to the celebration of the
>>first kiss,
>nurture us as we nurture the children in our lives.

From age to age, may we grow in faith

God of the generations,
>we come as heirs to your kingdom,
>standing on the shoulders of past generations,
>excited by the challenge set before us,
>yet humbled by your faith in us.

From age to age, may we grow in faith.

The United Reformed Church

Welcome to My World

>Tiny hands and tousled hair,
>lungs that gasp for gulps of air:
>as we hold you in our arms
>child-like innocence disarms.
>
>Star of darkness come to earth,
>child of joy we hymn your birth,
>child of hope for you we pray,
>light up this and every day.
>
>Caught within a wisp of time,
>all our reason, all our rhyme,
>fathoms depths of unknown scope,
>depths of love and human hope.

O what happiness we feel,
and this happiness is real!
God inspire each faltering phrase,
for this child sing out with praise!

Tune: Simplicity or Innocents

Andrew Pratt

Love – The Light of the World

A tiny spark you were
A scrap of life, a tiny baby,
And yet that spark was the light of the world.

And that tiny spark moved the world,
Shook it to its core,
Changed it forever.

That tiny spark
Shone light into the darkest places,
That tiny spark brought love and hope.
A love that was greater than anything ever known,
A love that lit a flame of hope
In the heart of humanity.

Love that flickered into life,
Love that was extinguished on the cross.
But love that could not be put out,
For in dying a brighter, bigger love became
A brighter light spread across the world.

Love – the tiny spark in a stable,
Love – the awesome gift of the cross,
Love – the light of the world,
Shining today for you and for me.

Debbie Hodge

281

Incarnation Prayer

Young women strap bombs on their bodies, looking very
   pregnant.
Corporations discard scientific evidence for profit's sake.
School children drive each other to suicide.
Tanks roll over cars and homes: this is my world.
Do you really deign to come into humanity now, O Prince of
   Peace?

My contemporary mind finds your nativity story
              – quite simply –
too cute   too quaint   too removed from what is real.

I am this 'Holy Night' appalled that any in tab and alb
Should glibly tell me you are born.
Or anyone with choir gown flowing
Should, comfy, sing, 'Joy to the earth, the saviour reigns . . .'

Yet I am drawn into our small church this Christmas Eve.
Do you weep with me, O Prince of Peace?
Was your great coming all in vain?

Suddenly, phrases once said so easily
stand starkly before me, huge granite rocks:
Prince of Peace   God of Love   Lord of Life

Yes, this I believe. Oh, help my unbelief!
For such a world as ours can only be saved by such a God as
   you.
It is our turn to cry, 'I thirst.' May that cry of the ancient
   Babe
well up in us this Holy Night and heart wrenching kyries.
Then hear our prayer and come to us. Abide with us.
O Prince of Peace, never go.

Betty Lynn Schwab
Canada

A New Song

Sing a new song for all the world,
God has kept his promise today,
peace on earth, goodwill to you all,
follow, follow, Christ leads the way.
Darkness fades in his shining light,
justice and joy are his delight,
nothing is hidden from his sight,
on the day that Jesus is born.

All creation welcomes the day,
cheering hills and rivers of praise,
blow the trumpet, ring the bells,
follow, follow, Christ leads the way.
Here is the child who is born to be king,
wonderful peace of which we sing,
what are the gifts that we can bring,
on the day that Jesus is born?

Let each carol echo with joy,
glory is the baby's name.
Jesus is the promise of God,
follow, follow, Christ leads the way.
Open the eyes that long to see,
unlock your heart and set it free,
be what God would like you to be,
on the day that Jesus is born.

Infant Jesus, born for the world,
God is lying in the hay,
born as one of the poor and oppressed,
follow, follow, Christ leads the way.
Lifting the low and raising the weak,
forgiving sin and healing the sick,
giving us power to dare to speak,
of the day that Jesus is born.

Colin Ferguson

Child in Need

It's Christmas time again
and the streets are full of people;
there are glittering decorations overhead,
music is playing 'Goodwill to all'
and bells are ringing from the steeple
while the crowds hurry by
their prayers unsaid.

It's Christmas time again
and the shops are selling madly
while carols are played by the Round Table
in the High Street. They sing 'Peace to all';
the poster child looks on sadly
as they rattle their collection tins
around a plastic stable.

It's Christmas time again
and the cash is flowing freely;
the shoppers carry on, heedless
as the loudspeaker bellows 'Love to all';
but this child has eyes that can only see the
pain and hunger that should
have been needless.

It's Christmas time again,
and in the midst of plenty
the bells are jingling on the shop's cash till
and the herald angels sing of 'Mercy for all'
but her heart and stomach remain empty
for where is her peace, mercy, love
or her goodwill?

It's Christmas time again
and the song is in the mind of those passing by.
The child is no longer a stranger
And we must sing for 'Justice for all';
our goodwill and peace, our mercy and love cry out
Glory for this child as well as
the child in the manger.

Colin Ferguson

Worlds Unknown

Word of flesh and Prince of Peace
child who is God's holy choice,
love can make the hatred cease,
worlds unknown shall yet rejoice.
Captive hearts find hope's release,
to the weak he gives a voice,
for our sins he weeps and bleeds,
      forgives us with dying voice,
      worlds unknown shall yet rejoice.

Sing of justice says the Lord,
let the people of my choice
now proclaim my living word,
worlds unknown shall yet rejoice.
Mercy given to the world,
loving gives my Spirit voice,
here today God's call is heard,
      those who listen are his choice,
      worlds unknown shall yet rejoice.

Hear the promise God still makes
through the channels of his choice,
light into the darkness breaks,
worlds unknown shall yet rejoice.

On this earth God makes his place,
justice frees the stricken voice,
all creation gives God praise,
    all the people are his choice,
    worlds unknown shall yet rejoice.

Colin Ferguson

Carol for the Prince of Peace

Do we need still more Christmas music?
LPs, tapes, cassettes, CDs and DVDs:
more and more come every year.
In shops and elevators, churches and halls
beginning in October: we hear it all again
and again – for the babe of an unknown mum.

Late this night, my computer showed me our world.
A suicide bomber strikes a distant crowded mall.
Our neighbourhood synagogue is firebombed.
One religious group is offended by another and kill in
    retaliation:
'Is peace possible?' is the week-long news special.

Making music in our era of terror must be hard work.
There can be no patience with the shallow sentiment or with
    the unfelt phrase.
A piano out of tune is far too much a symbol of our day.

Our music must be birthed laboriously from the anguish of
    our hearts.
Our music must be woven intricately from the overly
    abundant data in our minds.
Our music must be crafted meticulously from the confused
    longings of our souls.
We have not yet sung our Christmas carol
To the Prince of Peace.

Betty Lynn Schwab
Canada

O Sad and Troubled Bethlehem

O sad and troubled Bethlehem,
We hear your longing cry
For peace and justice to be born
And cruel oppression die.
How deep your need for that great gift
Of love in human form,
Let Christ in you be seen again
And hearts by hope made warm.

While morning stars and evening stars
Shine out in your dark sky,
Despair now stalks your troubled streets
Where innocents still die.
And Jesus, child of Mary,
Whose love will never cease,
Feels even now your pain and fear,
Longs with you for your peace.

Amazingly and lovingly
Jesus, the child, has come
And brought to birth through human pain,
Makes broken hearts his home.
He comes to comfort all who weep,
To challenge every wrong
And, living with the weak and poor,
Becomes their hope, their song.

Wendy Ross-Barker

We Searched for Peace

We searched for peace on planet earth
but it was difficult to find.
In Latin America people still suffered
from the after-effects of oppression.

In Africa there was a bitter legacy
from the days of colonialism.
In Europe the clouds of two world wars
hung heavy in the evening air.
So we journeyed to the holy land,
guided by a star, and came at last to Bethlehem.
There were tanks waiting on the village streets
and children with stones in their hands
and tears in their eyes.
Would that planet earth
knew the things that make for peace.
Return, Jesus, redeemer and saviour,
and show us how to find the blessing of peace.

John Johansen-Berg

Prince of Peace

Prince of Peace,
A world was prepared for your coming;
Prophets of old foretold you;
Spiritual seekers quietly awaited you.
In the fulfilment of time you came,
not with a fanfare of trumpets,
not with legions of soldiers to protect you,
not with a treasury of gold to finance you,
but in the earthiness of a stable,
in the vulnerable surroundings of a cradle,
with the crooning of a mother's song for welcome.
So you began your journey
from the cradle to the cross, costly vocation,
to redeem the world of sinners
and to establish peace on earth.

John Johansen-Berg

Mystery

What sort of world was it then
To enter into,
Forlorn and cold
With winter old and comfortless?
No place to be
Or reason that we
Know
To justify this priceless gift.

For who are we –
The greedy, shiftless, proud and mean
To merit bounty thus
In such complete entirety?

So who has watched us here,
Has seen our need
And heard our bitter battles,
And our feeble efforts at
Humanity?

Who looked at us
And saw a reason for redemption?
What love was this
To come in poverty
And darkness,
To have no place to be,
To suffer mockery
And death before due time?

What love is this
That came against the odds,
That still endures,
And with mysterious power
Redeems the irredeemable
For all infinity?

Margot Arthurton

Intercession at Christmas

(Selected verses to be used according to the situation of the local congregation)

We think of Joseph who must have been desperate to find somewhere to stay for the night.

We pray for the homeless people searching for shelter at this time of year. We pray that they will find your peace and welcome in unexpected places.

We think of Mary, expecting a baby any day now as she approaches Bethlehem.

We pray for people today who need professional care and who are unable to get it. We pray for people in the poor parts of the world who have to walk for many days to get to a doctor. We pray for people who cannot afford to pay for medical care or treatment.

We think of Jesus, being born in dirty, smelly, noisy conditions in a stable.

We pray for people living their lives in unhygienic unsanitary conditions. We pray for people whose water supply is a dirty pool, a mile from home.

We think of Mary and Joseph in Bethlehem, away from their friends and families.

We pray for people who are alone at Christmas and through-out the year. We pray for people who are bereaved – particularly people who have lost loved ones during the past year and who will be spending their first Christmas without them. We pray for people who have no friends, no family – and for folk whose families leave them behind at Christmas. We pray for the friendship groups, celebrating in (name your community) and elsewhere, thinking of the volunteers and the people who were not invited.

We think of Mary and Joseph and their new baby, fleeing from Herod into Egypt.

We pray for refugees today, running from threats of torture, from oppression, from war. We pray for refugees newly arrived in their new home, facing an uncertain future, having to fit in to a new culture and learn a new language.

We pray that as we prepare for, and celebrate, Christmas we are grateful to you for all that we have and especially for the gift of Jesus. Amen.

Alan Baldwin
England

Christ Mass Star

The brightness of a star,
the Christ mass star.
The light shone out,
a long time ago,

Shining to proclaim the birth of
The Prince of Peace,
Counsellor, Mighty One
at a placed called Bethlehem,

Shine on precious star of Bethlehem,
proclaiming hope for the future
for all the world to see
at Christmas time.

Shine on precious star of Bethlehem,
illuminate and again enlighten the world,
this Christmas time,
with your message of love.

Shine on for ever star of Bethlehem
proclaiming to the world
The Prince of Peace.
For the world today, tomorrow and for ever,

Barbara Oakes

Index of Authors

293

Index of Themes and Titles

Advent

Including the following themes:

Titles of each piece:

Christmas

Including the following themes:

Titles of each piece:

Epiphany

Including the following themes:

Titles of each piece:

301

Supplement of New Material

303

Acknowledgement and Sources

Every effort has been made to trace copyright ownership but the publisher would be grateful to know of any omissions.

Advent

Advent © Order of the Holy Paraclete

Advent Blessing (1) © Richard Becher

Advent Blessing (2) © Dorothy McRae-McMahon

Advent Candles © Revd John Johansen-Berg

Advent Candle Song © Christian Aid

Advent in the Convent © Revd John Johansen-Berg

Advent Prayer © Lesley K. Steel

After Me Comes Another . . . © Jill Jenkins

An Advent Candle Ceremony © Christian Aid

An Advent Eucharistic Prayer © Ann Lewin

Announcing © Revd John Johansen-Berg

As With Madness © Janet Lees

Blessing is not to be taken Lightly © Edmund Banyard from *Reaching the Infinite* published by the National Christian Education Council (NCEC). Used with Permission.

Bring Peace © Michael Perham for St George's Church, Oakdale.

Celebration in El Salvador © Christian Aid

Christmas Magic © Jan Berry

Christmas Rush © Ann Lewin published in *Candles and Kingfishers*.

Circles of Grace © from *Circles of Grace: Worship and Prayer in the Everyday* by Keri K. Wehlander. United Church Publishing House, 1998. Pages 12 and 13. Used with Permission.

Come Humbly, Holy Child © Mothers' Union

Come, Lord Jesus © Christian Aid

Come to Us, Lord Jesus Christ © Donald Hilton from *Pilgrim to the Holy Land* published by Mayhew McCrimmon. Used with Permission.

Coming for You, Coming for Me © Sun Ai Lee Park published as All the Broken Hearts in *In God's Image*, Asian Women's Resource Centre, Kuala Lumpur, Malaysia.

Conception © Frances Ballantyne

Expectation © Clare McBeath from *Justice, Joy and Jubilee*, the Prayer Handbook for 1999–2000, published by the United Reformed Church.

Follow the Light to Your Stable © Virginia Becher

For the Darkness and the Light © Janet Morley from *All Desires Known* published by SPCK. Used by permission.

Giving Time, A © Virginia Becher*

God of the Poor © Janet Morley, Christian Aid

Holy One © Janet Lees

How Long Does it Take to Make an Angel? © Fiona Ritchie Walker, Traidcraft

In Due Time © Frances Ballantyne

Litany for Advent, A © Keri K. Wehlander

Make Us Aware © Kate McIlhagga

Mary of Nazareth © Janet Lees

Mary's Lament © Margot Arthurton

May the Light of Justice Shine © Jan Berry

New Branch, The © Heather Pencavel

One Who Comes, The © Heather Pencavel

Our is a Biased God © Edmund Banyard from *Reaching for the Infinite* published by the National Christian Education Council (NCEC). Used with Permission.

Our Hope and our Desire © Janet Morley, Christian Aid

Posada Prayer © Garth Hewitt, Christian Aid, published in *Candle of Hope*, The Bible Reading Fellowship.

Prayer to the Christ Child, A © Christian Aid.

Prepare the Way of God © Michael Jacob Kooiman

Question © Wendy White

Ready Song, The © Jenny Dann

Christmas

Born Today © Peter Trow

Can You Hear the Angels Singing? © Peter Trow

Carol for Roshita, A © Barbara Moss

Carol of the Kingdom © Jill Jenkins

Celebrating Christmas © Louise Pirouet

Child is Missing, The © Heather Pencavel

Child of Bethlehem © Raymond Chapman from *Stations of the Nativity* published by The Canterbury Press. Used with Permission.

Christ Child, The © Jill Denison

Christ Like © Richard Becher

Christ our God © Janet Morley, Christian Aid

Christmas (1) © Anthea Dove

Christmas (2) © Paul Hampton

Christmas Baby, A © Derek Webster

Christmas Bells © Brian Louis Pearce

Christmas by the Roadside © Christian Aid

Christmas Card © Bernard Thorogood

Christmas Communion Liturgy, A © Peter Trow

Christmas Crib © Order of the Holy Paraclete

Christmas Day © Erna Colebrook from *A Spark in My Soul*

Christmas Eve © Revd John Johansen-Berg

Christmas Eve Thanksgiving, A © Derek Webster

Christmas in Nazareth from © *A Continent Called Palestine* by Najwa Farah, published by SPCK Publishing.

Christmas in the Southern Hemisphere © W. L. Wallace

Christmas is a Time for . . . © Jason Doré

Christmas Meditation © James Ashdown

Christmas Prayer, A © by Robert Stark from *Worship for All Seasons Vol 1 Advent, Christmas and Epiphany*, edited by Thomas Harding. The United Church Publishing House, 1993, p. 71. Reprinted with Permission.

Christmas Prayer for Peace, A © Christian Aid

Christmas Prayer of Confession, A © by Gordon Nodwell from *Worship for All Seasons Vol 1 Advent, Christmas and Epiphany*, edited by Thomas Harding. The United Church Publishing House, 1993, pp. 71 & 72. Reprinted with Permission.

Christmas Rap, The © Christian Aid

Christmas Samaritan, The © Richard Becher

Christmas Tide © Kate McIlhagga

Christmas Time © Frances Ballantyne

Christmas Welcome © Stephen Brown from *Gateways of Grace*, the Prayer Handbook for 1998–1999, published by the United Reformed Church.

Come, Christmas God © Kate McIlhagga

Cradled-Christ Eucharist © Revd Susan Hardwick, an Anglican priest and author of a number of books.

Crisis at Christmas © Revd John Johansen-Berg

Family of Christ, The © Revd Susan Hardwick, an Anglican priest and author of a number of books.

For the Rich and the Poor © Goodwin Zainga

Gift, The © Heather Johnston

Gift of Peace, A © Richard Becher

Give Thanks to God © Peter Trow

God Born as a Baby © Jan Berry

God With Us © Edmund Banyard from *Reaching the Infinite* published by the National Christian Education Council (NCEC). Used with Permission.

Gospel Reflection, A © W. L. Wallace

Harassed, Haunted Child of Mary, Andrew Pratt © Stainer and Bell

He's Grown, That Baby, originally published © Incarnation by Ann Lewin published in *Candles and Kingfishers*.

Here at Last © Heather Pencavel

Herod's High and Mighty Stand, Andrew Pratt © Stainer and Bell

How Far is It to Bethlehem? © Kate Compston

308

How I'll Spend This Christmas © Fiona Ritchie Walker, Traidcraft

If Only . . . © Richard Becher

Incarnation © Revd Susan Hardwick, an Anglican priest and author of a number of books.

Incarnation of Christ for the Entire World, The – Aspects from Palestine © Rt Revd Riah Abu El-Assal

Inside Out? © Peter Trow

It is Dark Outside and Very Cold © Oriole and Art Veldhuis

Joselie's Dream © Christian Aid

Joy Abounding © Revd John Johansen-Berg

Korean Welcome, A © Christian Aid

Let there be Light © Christian Aid

Let Us Go and See © Goodwin Zainga

Let's Go to Bethlehem © Peter Radcliffe/Jubilate Hymns. Tune: Zither Carol (Girls and boys). (*Carols for Choirs, Junior Praise 2, The Popular Carol Book*).

Light Has Come, The © Melanie Frew from *Justice, Joy and Jubilee*, the Prayer Handbook for 1999–2000, published by the United Reformed Church.

Litany on a New Year's Eve © Sinfonia Oecumenica

Love Came Down at Christmas © Heather Pencavel

Miracle and Magic © Heather Pencavel

Nativity, A © Derek Webster

Nativity Gift List © Heather Johnston

Nativity Now © Jill Jenkins

New-Born, The © Revd Alan Gaunt

No Room: We're Full © Louise Pirouet

Northumbrian Nativity © Kate McIlhagga

Not One Advent © Bernard Thorogood

Now is the Time, the Time of God's Favour © Christopher Idle. Published with the author's permission.

On Christmas Day © Paul Hampton

On the Eve of Christmas © Sabeel Liberation Theology Centre

Our Lady of the Refugees – Source Unknown

Pass-the-Parcel Love: A Christmas Gift © Revd Susan Hardwick, an Anglican priest and author of a number of books.

Post Communion Prayer for Christmas Eve or Christmas Day © Revd Alan Gaunt

Pray for Peace © Christian Aid

Prayer for Christmas Eve, A (1) © Revd Alan Gaunt

Prayer for Christmas Eve, A (2) © Revd Alan Gaunt

Prayer of Confession for Christmas Eve, A © Revd Alan Gaunt

Prayers – Reflecting on Christmas © Heather Pencavel

Prayers Around a Nativity Scene © Christian Aid

Prayers of Intercession (1) © Heather Pencavel

Prayers of Intercession (2) © Heather Pencavel

Scandalous God © Kate Compston

Seeing the Christmas Christ – December in an African Prison © c/o The Canterbury Press

Shining Lights © Christian Aid

Silent Night © Lesley K. Steel

Sing till Sundown © Eileen Spinelli. Permission sought.

Someone Who has become a Friend © Glenn Jetta Barclay

Sometimes I Cry © Kathy Galloway from *Love Burning Deep* published by SPCK Publishing.

Sort of Bethlehem, A © Brian Louis Pearce

Southern Christmas © Bernard Thorogood

Star Light © Revd John Johansen-Berg

Stars and Angels © Heather Pencavel

Suleiman Family, The © Christian Aid

Tale of the Innkeeper © R. May Hill

The Shining Stars Unnumbered © in Europe and the Commonwealth (excluding Canada) by Timothy Dudley-Smith and in the rest of the world by Hope Publishing Company, Carol Stream, IL 60188, USA.

Time for Welcoming the Prince of Peace, A © Revd John Johansen-Berg

Unwrap the Gift © Virginia Becher*

Visit to Reading Prison on Christmas Day, A © Dominic Walker

Vulnerable God © Jan Berry

Wake Up, A Christmas Card, Chile © Christian Aid

Was There No Other Way? © Edmund Banyard from *Reaching the Infinite* published by the National Christian Education Council (NCEC). Used with Permission.

We Kneel © Kate McIlhagga

We, too, are Shepherds © Wendy White

Welcome © Fiona Liddell

What's on Tonight? © Heather Pencavel

What Star shall We Follow? © Rebecca Dudley, Christian Aid

When the Child was Born © 2000 Louise Margaret Granahan

Why Them? © Ann Lewin published in *Candles and Kingfishers*.

Winter Solstice © Kate McIlhagga

Wonderful Counsellor – Prayer taken from *The Promise of His Glory* is copyright © The Central Board of Finance 1990, 1991; The Archbishop's Council, 1999 and is reproduced by permission.

World in Pain, A Baby's Cry, A © Christopher Idle

Yesterday's News © Peter Trow

Your Word Made Flesh © Norm S. D. Esdon

*Virginia Becher travelled a very painful Advent journey during 1999. She died on 1 January 2000 after being in a coma throughout Christmas 1999.

Epiphany

An Epiphany Prayer (1) © Joan McMurtry. Used with permission.

An Epiphany Prayer (2) © Gail Ramshaw. Used with permission.

Baptism of Christ, The © W. L. Wallace

Christ from Heaven's Glory Come © in the UK, Europe and Africa by Timothy Dudley-Smith and in the rest of the world by Hope Publishing Company, Carol Stream, IL 60188, USA.

Christ the Door © W. L. Wallace

Christmas Cards © Louise Pirouet

Epiphanic Arrival of the Camel-Drivers © Anne Richards

Epiphany © Kate McIlhagga

Epiphany Hymn © Jan Berry

Eucharist Prayer © Ann Lewin

Flight into Egypt © Raymond Chapman from *Stations of the Nativity*, published by The Canterbury Press.

God at Epiphany © Julie M. Hulme

God by Extension © Stephen Brown from *Gateways of Grace*, the Prayer Handbook for 1998–1999, published by the United Reformed Church.

God, in Whom is Peace © Jan Berry

God of Life © *Circles of Grace: Worship and Prayer in the Everyday* by Keri K. Wehlander. United Church Publishing House, 1998, p. 108. Used with Permission.

Here Stands A Stranger, Who Is She? Andrew Pratt © Stainer and Bell

Invocation to the Christ of the Four Directions © Suzanne Fageol

Joseph's Story from a homily by Rt Revd S. Tilewa Johnson, Bishop of Gambia, from *On Frequent Journeys; Worship Resources on Uprooted Peoples*, edited by Rebekah Chevalier. © The United Church Publishing House, 1997, p. 108.

Journeying Magi's Mood-Swings, A © Revd Susan Hardwick, an Anglican priest and author of a number of books.

Jubilee © Kate Compston

Let Every Word © Dom Helder Camara

Litany for Refugees and Asylum Seekers, A © Louise Pirouet

Living, Loving God © Geoff Duncan

Lord, We Pray for those Living on the Edge of Communities – Rachel Lampard and Jennie Richmond © Catholic Housing Aid Society

Magi, The © Paul Hampton

Magi's Pilgrimage: Found © Kate Compston

Mary and Joseph Came to the Temple, Andrew Pratt © Stainer and Bell

On Offering a Reflection for Christmas © Heather Pencavel

Our Common Baptism © Sinfonia Oecumenica

Parable of A Christmas Banquet, The © Richard Becher

Pilgrimage © W. L. Wallace

Praise to You, Son of the Most High © Ephrem of Syria

Prayers for Refugees © Jesuit Refugee Service

Presentation in the Temple, The from *A Year with Mary* © Elizabeth Obbard adapted by Geoff Duncan.

Recognise and Respond © Heather Johnston from *Active Power*, the Prayer Handbook for 1998, published by the United Reformed Church.

Rise within Us like a Star © Kate Compston

Setting Out © Janet Wootton from *Journeying*, the Prayer Handbook for 1997, published by the United Reformed Church.

Setting Out on the Pilgrim Way © Sinfonia Oecumenica

Shine On © Garth Hewitt Chain of Love Music

Simeon © Anthea Dove

Soft the Evening Shadows Fall © in Europe, the UK and Africa by Timothy Dudley-Smith and in the rest of the world by Hope Publishing Company, Carol Stream, IL 60188, USA.

Star, The © W. L. Wallace

Star of Bethlehem © Revd John Johansen-Berg

Through Darkness the Light Still Shines © Edmund Banyard from *Reaching the Infinite*, published by the National Christian Education Council (NCEC). Used with Permission.

Travelling On © Jan Berry, Journeying in Hope from *Gateways of Grace*, the Prayer Handbook for 1998–1999, published by the United Reformed Church.

Wise Words for the Epiphany Season © Brendan Walsh

Supplement of New Material

Candle, The © Barbara Oakes, Ashton-in-Makerfield

Carol for the Prince of Peace © Betty Lynn Schwab

Child in Need © Colin Ferguson

Christ Mass Star © Barbara Oakes, Ashton-in-Makerfield

Expectation © from *Justice, Joy and Jubilee*, the Prayer Handbook for 1999–2000, published by the United Reformed Church

Heirs to the Kingdom © from *Justice, Joy and Jubilee*, the Prayer Handbook for 1999–2000, published by the United Reformed Church

Incarnation Prayer © Betty Lynn Schwab

Intercessions at Christmas © Alan Baldwin

Love – The Light of the World © Debbie Hodge

Magnificat for Three Choirs © Ann Lewin from *Flashes of Brightness*

Mystery © Margot Arthurton

New Song, A © Colin Ferguson

O Sad and Troubled Bethlehem © Wendy Ross-Barker

Prince of Peace © John Johansen-Berg

We Searched for Peace © John Johansen-Berg

Welcome to My World, Andrew Pratt © Stainer and Bell

Worlds Unknown © Colin Ferguson